At the Feet of my Master

The Oneness
of
An ascending heart-cry
And
A descending Soul-Smile

Pradhan Balter

Copyright©2010, by Pradhan Balter

Pubisher:
Retlab Inc.
    3406 N. Hoyne Ave.
    Chicago, IL 60618

All rights reserved. No portion of this book may be reproduced in any form without the express written permission of the author.

Cover: Bird-drawings and handwritten title by Sri Chinmoy.

Writings by Sri Chinmoy reprinted with permission of Agni Press and AUM Publications.

Inquiries, comments, questions:
Pradhan Balter
c/o Retlab Inc.
3406 N. Hoyne Ave.
Chicago, IL 60618
pradhan@pradhanb.com

Special thanks go to my friends who encouraged me in writing this book. In particular, I would like to mention Tanima, Priyadarshan and Aditi for their wonderful support!

ISBN-9780982506103

At the Feet of my Master

Introduction 3

The Early Days 5
- ❖ Coming to the path
- ❖ Smile from the soul
- ❖ The inward-facing blessing pin
- ❖ "My ego is killing me"
- ❖ The damage cured
- ❖ "Your poem is so beautiful"
- ❖ A confirmation of Guru's vision

"Pop" 21
- ❖ A painful generation gap revisited
- ❖ My father's heart begins to melt
- ❖ Sarama's house
- ❖ Chiropractic school or medical school
- ❖ Tumors don't read textbooks
- ❖ A generation gap dissolved…and then some!
- ❖ "I'm so glad you're home"
- ❖ September 1, 1976–receiving my name
- ❖ Receiving my pink slip

My Father's Passing 33
- ❖ I am your Eternity's father
- ❖ Two fathers
- ❖ Your father was here

At the Feet of my Master 41
- ❖ NOAMS: No Outer Attention Misery Syndrome
- ❖ Appearances
- ❖ "So Ron has left"
- ❖ "I am leaving the Centre"
- ❖ "Just who am I working on?"
- ❖ Guru's pain and Ongkar's pain
- ❖ Making faces
- ❖ Ongkar's passing
- ❖ What's in Guru's back pocket?
- ❖ Running into a cop during the NYC Marathon

Sagas from the Concert World 61
- ❖ The concert challenge (part 1)
- ❖ I would go there myself
- ❖ The concert challenge (part 2)
- ❖ Humility is the key
- ❖ The 1992 concert
- ❖ The 1993 concert
- ❖ The 27,000 concert (part 1)
- ❖ The 27,000 concert (part 2)
- ❖ The squirrel and the crow
- ❖ A spiritual transfusion

The Great Pizza Wars 77
- ❖ "What, no pizza?"
- ❖ The Venezuela pizza experience
- ❖ The Mormon pizza experience
- ❖ One piece of pizza, one new student
- ❖ "Chicago pizza is by far the best!"
- ❖ "I like it much better"

Guru-isms **85**
- Guru's sweater gift
- Don't hide when you make mistakes
- "I am a real tiger"
- "Just be happy"
- Be careful what you say!
- Guru's 50th birthday nap
- Be a weightlifter

Scoldings **91**
- On scoldings
- One million lifetimes
- My first scolding
- "You will get your realization from this"
- The three-month "vacation"
- The 3-elevator stop scolding (part 1): Guru's words can burn your heart
- The 3-elevator stop scolding (part 2): Guru's words can melt your heart
- The student's oneness
- China

The Final Chapter **123**
- "You belong to me"

Dedicated Eternally to my Beloved Guru

On October 11, 2007, my Master—my Beloved Guru—left this physical world. While he is no longer with me physically, his inner presence remains a constant beacon for my life. In New York, a special memorial is erected at his burial site. I visit this site regularly. It is brilliant with Guru's spiritual force—a force which reinforces and sustains me in my spiritual practice. This book is dedicated to him.

Once, after a mild and light-hearted reprimand, Guru smiled most affectionately said to me, "It will take you one million lifetimes to realize how much love I have for you." This is one, Guru; just 999,999 to go...

1

Introduction

As I began writing these stories, an interesting thing happened. While thinking back to past experiences, small, seemingly less significant recollections came forward. These little recollections seemed to "connect" the bigger ones to create a pattern of experiences which had value. Interestingly, I could actually trace these recollections back to a time before I became Sri Chinmoy's student! For example, in planning these stories, I had no intention of talking about the drug experience which almost killed me and left me very damaged (which preceded my becoming a student) until I recalled that it was Sri Chinmoy (Guru, as all of his students call him) who cured me of the residual damage. Was Guru there too?

I have heard Guru say that none of his students came to him accidentally. Although I would accept this as a philosophical reality, the process of recalling and connecting these now brought this into the realm of a very joyful realization. On a regular basis, I massaged Guru's always pained legs, and, as it happened, I had

Introduction

the opportunity to work on Guru within minutes of having this realization. Guru was seated in his chair, and when I walked into his area, he looked at my smiling face and immediately said, "Pradhan, what?"

"Guru, may I ask you a question?" His raised brow indicated a "Yes"; so I explained my experience. "Guru, as I look back to write these stories, it seems to me that you were actually present and operating in my life before I became a student!"

"It is absolutely true," Guru commented. "My spiritual children think that they come to a class, or see me for the first time and then they become students. But I have a third eye! Long before they saw me, with my inner vision I was calling their souls towards me."

I have also heard Guru say that once we are accepted as students, he is in charge of our past, present and future. This is very good because, if I were in charge, I would only make a mess of it. In fact, that's what this collection of stories has made me realize–that basically my life has become a game in which I do an excellent job of making a mess of it, while Guru has the formidable task of setting it straight!

In narrating these stories I have attempted to apply some framework–for example, a chronology or a theme. Some of the stories are just moments of Guru being Guru; others are experiences and reflections; while others are lessons that may have transpired over a period of years. I do hope that they provide some joy, a bit of inspiration and perhaps a little glimpse into one student's relationship with his Guru.

2

The Early Days

❖ **Coming to the path**

I first started my own spiritual processing in the late sixties/early seventies. This, some of you may recall, is when the whole yoga-meditation thing first became popular with the hippie movement and the Beatles' trip to India. That era was very turbulent in terms of social change in America: Nixon was president, the war in Viet Nam was being fought in our living rooms, Watergate was being exposed, cities were being burned down and drugs were in broad and popular use among young people.

I was absorbed in the drug/hippie culture, initiated by my older brother Lenny—definitely one of those emulation things. Whatever he did, I followed suit.

Although there is much more to my story as a hippie, what is relevant to this discourse is that I nearly died from a drug overdose. I unintentionally took an immense amount of a weird concoction of drugs that nearly killed me.

The Early Days

For two days after, I fell in and out of a black sleep. Finally, I woke up feeling that I was going to be all right, and asked for something to eat. Yes, I was all right, but the experience left me changed.

For one thing, I really damaged some brain cells. I would regularly and completely lose my train of thought in mid-sentence. This was particularly painful for me, because I was born with an innate gift of conversation. Secondly, I was left genuinely paranoid and fear-filled.

Interestingly, this happened at a time when I was just beginning to explore hatha yoga, and as a result had actually decided to stop my drug use, but the overdose kicked me out of the drug lifestyle for good. My friends tried to get me back into taking drugs, but every attempt sent fear rushing through me. Finally, and most importantly, the experience left me with a tremendous sense of gratitude that I was still alive, and with that, a quiet question—why did I choose life? What was there about life that I had clung to it so desperately?

I want to put this into proper perspective. I have always been and remain, gratefully, a pretty emotionally stable person—rarely get angry, always considerate of others, well-liked. During this experience, I did not have any divine revelations or anything like that. It is simply that my entire framework of life was jolted. At the time of the experience, I would only describe it as absolutely harrowing, but now I look back on it with gratitude. The experience took me off one road and put me on to another, which has proven to be much more fulfilling. At the time, I had no idea what that road was going to be, but the process was gently driven by the "why life?" issue.

When this overdose experience happened, I was still enrolled at Northwestern University. My natural tendency in education was toward mathematics and the sciences. In fact, I transferred out of Liberal Arts into Engineering School. It was always a struggle to write, but I could "add like hell". I still consider myself of the "scientific" mode.

Recall also that this whole ordeal occurred when I was getting into hatha yoga. In hindsight, this synchronicity of events and influences in my life seems more than a coincidence.

I was performing my hatha yoga exercises quite regularly and enjoying them very much. Soon I was doing hatha yoga about two hours a day, which inspired an interest in the philosophical aspects of yoga. I bought a book called *How to Know God: Patanjali's Yogic Aphorisms*. At that time, I wasn't into God at all, but I was into yoga, and here was a simple book on the philosophy of yoga by an Indian named Swami Prabhavananda.

This book was a dramatic contrast for me. First of all, I was not a big reader, and when I did read, it was a scientific journal or article. But here I was reading a philosophy book—on "Eastern" philosophy no less. Well, that book was remarkable and had a profound effect on me. Here was a wonderful life philosophy, more complete than anything I could conceive of by myself, or had ever heard of in any Western psychologies. Its words affirmed themselves with me and I continually found myself nodding "yes". It spoke of an intimate relationship between man and God. This was a different God from the one that I had been taught about in the Jewish faith. This was a God that existed inside me—my own highest self. For some reason, this resonated with me. Swami Prabhavananda spoke of the "inner life", and the role of the spiritual Teacher and how the Teacher serves the aspiration of the seeker.

I read about a very special category of spiritual Teacher—the *Avatar*, the divine incarnation. Of course, we in the West are familiar with the Christ as such a Teacher, but here I read the names of Buddha, Krishna and Ramakrishna alongside that of the Christ. Now, having been raised in the Jewish faith, this was all relatively foreign to me, but it was so compelling that I was convinced of the *possibility* that it was true. The God it defined was a God I could deal with, a God who lived inside me, and was my own higher nature. Frankly, this book inspired me tremendously. I still reread it from time to time.

The Early Days

At Northwestern, I also began to change direction in my education. I was a senior at the time and had already completed my engineering curricula. I was required to take some courses in the humanities to round out my education, so I took advantage of this to continue my "why life?" investigation. I took a course in Buddhism, studying the *Dhammapada* with a Buddhist monk.

On my own time I dabbled in many of the great scriptures. I read the *Ramayana*, the *Mahabharata* and the *Bhagavad Gita*. I studied bits and pieces of the *Upanishads* and the *Vedas*.

I read a book called *Ramakrishna and His Disciples* by Christopher Isherwood and had a wonderful experience. As I turned the pages, while reading certain passages the sweetest fragrance seemed to come off the pages. My hair would stand on end and tears would spontaneously well up. I was filled with a great sense of joy. This came entirely unexpectedly.

And then I took a giant leap for someone raised in the Jewish faith—I read most of the New Testament. In the Jewish faith you just don't believe in the Christ as the Christians do. As a Jew I'd hear things like "he was a nice man", or "he was a great teacher", or even "he really didn't exist". But in no way, shape or form was he "The Messiah". So to read the New Testament was indeed a giant leap.

Wonderfully, I was greeted with the same experiences as when I read about Ramakrishna. Again, fragrance would rise off the pages and tears would well up in my eyes. That experience left me with a profound and intimate link with the Christ. (Many people have suggested that I must have been a priest in a previous lifetime!)

Here it's important to clarify that I was raised not necessarily "believing" in any one thing. I was not brought up to believe in any kind of conscious spiritual process at all, save for that of being a moral and good human being. My religious rearing as a Jew was, for the most part, a socio-cultural thing. I would call myself more "Jew-ish" than Jewish. And certainly, the concept that there is *only one way* of spiritual practice was completely foreign to me! Quite the contrary. My Jewish upbringing was such that I was quite tolerant and open to all sorts of possibilities.

What I witnessed in all this reading was very important. Here were 10,000 years of recorded spiritual histories that were all saying basically the same thing—10,000 years! They may have said it for a different time and a different culture, but the essence of what they were all saying was the same. This was in stark contrast to my scientific training that was constantly in the process of disproving itself. When I began my physics studies at Northwestern, I started studying Newton and his falling apple. Before leaving Northwestern, I was studying Einstein's physics which explain that Newton's physics were a good approximation, but wrong.

This is very consistent with the nature of science. Science is always in the process of discounting its previously accepted truths. At one time the earth was the center of the universe. Now, of course, we know that the earth rotates around the sun. Just recently I viewed a documentary from the late 1950s on the essence of a good diet: morning bacon and eggs fried in lots of butter, with white toast, smothered in more butter...mmm. How different the prescribed scientific diet is today! Ironically, no matter what day, year or era, science admits "well that was then, but *now* we know..."

But here was 10,000 years of recorded spiritual experience and history, and the truths and teachings spoken of remained essentially the same over time. This suggested to me that all these Teachers and learned men must have been tapping into the same source. It was enough to convince me to investigate further.

One thing all the Teachers addressed was the necessity and role of the Teacher. Because every scripture addressed the necessity of a Teacher, I was convinced that I should have one. After all, if Ramakrishna, the Buddha and the Christ all were influenced by spiritual Teachers in their formative rediscovery, it

The Early Days

didn't take a whole lot of humility on my part to think I could probably use one.

When I returned to my home in New York from Northwestern, I started my search for a Teacher. I contacted every yoga organization in New York City. Trust me, they are *all* there! Upon receiving literature from the various organizations I contacted, I was regularly greeted by two things: one was what I call the "sage look"—a smiling, long-haired bearded man. Well, I already had the sage look myself, so that didn't impress me. The second thing was a fee, which was a complete turn-off. It just intuitively struck me as wrong. Look at the great Teachers. When did they ever charge a fee?

The last place I contacted was called **Yoga of Westchester**. Now, I have to tell you that based on the name alone, this was the last place I ever expected to find a meditation class or Teacher. Westchester is, in large part, upper-middle class. I anticipated that Yoga of Westchester would be a group of house-moms who got together, stood on their heads and then had tea! (PLEASE forgive my political incorrectness.) When I called, I was greeted by a very nice woman. She had an Indian name, Sarama, which was the first of many Westerners with Indian names I would soon meet. I asked her about meditation, and she informed me that

"if you would like to meditate with a genuine Master of the highest caliber, Sri Chinmoy is offering a free meditation at Columbia University." Well, "free" was the thing that caught me, and so I went.

If you're expecting some cosmic tale at this point about my experience, you'll be disappointed. I attended that meditation with a friend. It was okay, but I wasn't particularly impressed. I was handed a brochure on Sri Chinmoy and meditation. I sat in the back of a large auditorium. There were all varieties of people there—young, old, nuns, hippies and more. About ten minutes was all that I could take. I left with my friend, bought a bottle of

The Early Days

Mateus wine and sipped the evening away in Central Park. So much for the cosmic, spiritual experience!

It turns out that **Yoga of Westchester** was the closest yoga center to my home and I decided to take hatha yoga classes there. Sarama's yoga studio was punctuated with pictures of Sri Chinmoy. In my various readings, the appearance of someone who was meditating in a high consciousness was described— the eyes half-closed, seemingly looking in and yet looking out. Sri Chinmoy *had* that appearance.

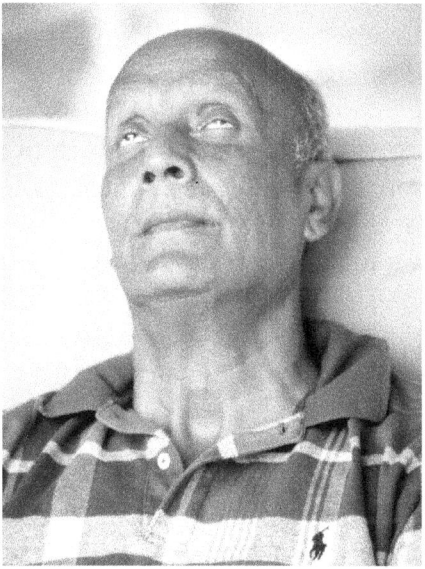

This is one of my favorite photos: Guru is in a very high meditation, and he is wearing a very nice Polo shirt! It is an icon for me, of sorts, saying that the inner life and the outer life can go together. Whenever I give classes on meditation, I always have this photo present!

Before this, I had never witnessed anyone who fit that description. There was no question in my mind that he was experiencing some states of consciousness beyond the everyday. And it was based on this simple academic recognition that I decided to find out what he was about. I was going to give him three months to show me what he knew.

The Early Days

I started by reading Sri Chinmoy's books and meditating as he prescribed. It seemed to work. In order to facilitate the inner link between the Teacher and student, a special photograph taken of Sri Chinmoy in a very high meditation is used. This particular photograph of Sri Chinmoy is referred to as "the Transcendental." Now, it is only given to those who are formally students of Sri Chinmoy, but in those days, the Transcendental was given out to anyone who requested it. I used it and noted a qualitative shift in my meditation. After a month or so I decided to formally become a student.

It was the fall of 1971. In those days, in order to become a student, you had a personal interview with Guru. Guru lived in a simple, modest home in Queens, NY. I arrived there not knowing quite what to expect. As I approached the front door, Guru was there to greet me. He opened the door and, with a gesture from his hand, indicated I should come in.

I didn't know quite what to do, but again with a gesture he indicated I should sit down. Guru took his seat, facing me. Somewhat at a loss for the appropriate words, I said nothing. (I mean, just what do you say to a "God-Realized Master"?) He simply requested, "Please look at me", which I did. Guru began to meditate on me. I watched Guru's eyes as they moved back and forth rapidly and penetratingly. I could see from his facial expression that he seemed to be inwardly climbing and searching. As he directed that meditative gaze towards me, I was overcome with the distinct feeling that he was looking right through me, and as he did so, that he knew me completely. It was just an impression, but one I couldn't ignore.

His meditation ended and, in the Indian tradition, he bowed to me with folded hands, a bow which I returned. Then he asked quite casually, "Your parents won't mind you doing this?"

"No," I responded, somewhat surprised that he would even ask. My parents had experienced four sons' worth of mischief and seemed to handle it all with more than enough aplomb. I couldn't imagine they would mind me doing this.

Then Guru reiterated, "Your mother won't mind?"

Now I responded with a "correcting" tone. "No, my mother would *never* mind," thinking to myself that perhaps my father might mind, but never my mother. My father was in the process of rediscovering his own Judaic roots subsequent to his mother's recent passing. He was attending temple quite regularly, so I could anticipate him possibly suggesting that I try the temple instead. But the thought of my mother minding was inconceivable... never.

"Fine," Guru replied. As I departed, Guru escorted me to his front door saying, "Come tonight. If you please me, then you may continue to come."

"I will please you," I replied with utmost confidence. What audacity! I officially began this journey in early 1971. I began it having read much and thinking I knew a lot. Now, some thirty-eight years later, I *know* that I know very little, but at least I am confident in that little knowledge!

❖ Smile from the soul

After receiving that first interview with Guru, I attended meditation that same evening. Upon arriving at Guru's home, I was grateful to be greeted by a few kind people, but in general the entire affair was a bit foreign to me. In those days, we meditated in Guru's living room. Chairs were set up facing the front porch. Guru sat in the front facing us.

At a certain point Guru invited each of us to show him our "soul's smile". He went downstairs, which was then a large library, and sat at a small table at the base of the stairway, while each of us filed downstairs one at a time. I, frankly, had no idea what I was doing. I remembered going down the steps, standing in front of Guru and smiling. Guru said something like, "Very good!" and I turned around to return upstairs. As I climbed the steps, it happened. Guru gave me the experience. A smile came over my face that was so broad it was almost painful, and with it came an ethereal beauty that permeated the entire atmosphere.

The Early Days

I made it back to my chair and all I could do was look around, smile and repeat, "Beautiful, beautiful, beautiful."

One by one, Guru gave each of us this experience, and by the time the last person returned from downstairs, the entire room was filled with beaming faces.

After that, Guru himself returned upstairs, took his seat at the front of the room and then demonstrated various smiles, all of which were aspects of the "soul's smile". In doing so, he took it upon himself to keep each person beaming. If he noticed someone's smile start to droop, he would direct his concentrated gaze at them until their smile returned.

When the meditation was over, I ran to my car and returned to my home as quickly as I could. I entered our apartment and couldn't wait to tell my mother about my experience. "Mom, you're not going to believe this! You're not going to believe this!" And then I went on to tell her about my experience.

I was right–she didn't believe it.

❖ The inward-facing blessing pin

After being accepted as a student, one received a special "Blessing Pin". The image on the pin was a picture of Guru in a very high meditation, and it came with specific instructions for meditation. This was quite ceremonial. Guru would call you up, meditate with you, and then offer this special pin. With the boys, Guru would actually pin the Blessing Pin over your heart.

When it came time for me to receive my Blessing Pin, as with the other boys, Guru pinned it on my shirt. Of course, since I was facing Guru, I couldn't actually see Guru pinning it on. When I finally did see it, Guru had apparently folded back the buttoned portion of my shirt in such a way that the pin was actually placed on the inside of the shirt facing inwards toward my chest, as opposed to being on the outside of my shirt facing outwards as everybody else's pin. I was certain this meant that Guru was embarrassed to have me as his student.

The Early Days

❖ "My ego is killing me"

Early on, there were three main Centres around the New York area: New York, Connecticut and New Jersey. In those days, these Centres actually met in their respective states and Guru would travel to each Centre on a weekly basis. As part of being accepted as a student, Guru would assign you to a Centre. There was a hierarchy of sorts attached to this assignment. The New York Centre students met twice a week on Thursday evenings and Sunday afternoons. Additionally, New York students could attend the other two Centre meetings in Connecticut and New Jersey. The Connecticut students met Monday evenings and could attend the New Jersey meetings. The New Jersey students met on Tuesday evenings at Fairleigh Dickinson University. That was their only evening to see Guru.

At any rate, I never spoke with Guru back then. Occasionally he would walk around, sort of mingle and greet people. One evening at Fairleigh Dickinson, he was descending the steps of the auditorium. When he passed me, he kindly asked of me, "You are all right?"

Trying to say something significant, I replied, "Oh, I'm fine, Guru, but my ego is killing me."

❖ The damage cured

When I became Sri Chinmoy's student, I was living in New York with my parents, but was still enrolled at Northwestern University. I was in a special program in the Engineering School in which you worked for part of the school year and hence completed your curriculum in five years instead of the standard four. I still had six months of school remaining, and so in December of 1971, I left New York to finish school.

Upon returning to my room in Chicago, the very first thing I did was to set up my meditation shrine. I had just completed this task when one of my apartment mates, Mark Wolf, rushed into my room. "Balter, how's it going...are you okay?" He was referring to my drug experience which he had heard about. Apparently, the fact that I had nearly died of an overdose made its way through the clique of friends in Chicago who were my "drug mates" as well as school mates.

I began to recollect the experience for him. Previous to this time, each time I would speak about my drug experience, I would literally relive it with a fear that was so intense I would be shaking by the end of the story. Also, as I mentioned earlier, the experience burned out some brain cells, often causing me to lose my train of thought completely in mid-sentence. And I do mean *lose*. I'd be saying something and suddenly there would be a pause followed by, "What was I talking about?" This residual manifestation had been happening repeatedly in my speech pattern, and was foreign, painful and embarrassing to me.

But as I related my story to Mark, something else happened. Mark and I were sitting in front of the newly constructed shrine. The Transcendental (remember, the special meditation photograph) was a few feet from me. As I retold the experience, waves of light and joy were coming from the Transcendental. (Really! I am not prone to this sort of experience.) And as these waves came towards me, there was no more fear, and from that moment on the damage was gone. My thoughts were no longer interrupted and I could speak coherently once more. Some of my brother and sister students might even suggest that perhaps Guru overcorrected!

❖ **"Your poem is so beautiful"**

I was on my own while at Northwestern. There were no other students of Sri Chinmoy there but I did okay...not great, but okay. I carried with me the excitement and inspiration of a new meditation student. Believe it or not, I used to get up almost every day at 4:30 a.m. to practice japa. Japa is a spiritual discipline of repeating a chant hundreds and hundreds of times.

I would occasionally receive letters from a childhood friend who also had become a student of Guru's at the same time as I had. One letter that I received I will never forget. My friend told

The Early Days

me Guru had requested that the boys wear whites and the girls wear saris for meditation functions. You see, Guru's spiritual path as it now stands was just beginning to evolve. I hope it's safe to say that Guru was experimenting with what was needed for a Western culture with which he wasn't completely familiar, a culture that was hardly prepared for genuine spiritual aspiration.

Sarama (yes...the same woman who first answered my initial phone call to Yoga of Westchester) served as the intermediary for my connection with Guru. In those days, she was an excellent photographer and took many wonderful photos of Sri Chinmoy. To this day, some of her photographs remain absolutely immortal. One particular album that she produced was called the "High Consciousness" album. It contained a number of photos of Guru meditating, representing a number of extremely high states of consciousness. When you bought this album, Guru signed it with your name. I bought it upon my departure from New York for Chicago. "Sandy" was written on the front page of the album in Guru's own hand. (At that point, I had not yet received my spiritual name. Sandy was my family nickname.)

I would look at this album quite often, and one day wrote a simple poem about it. I mailed it off to Guru's home address.

A few weeks later I received a letter with a return address of Jamaica, Queens on it. I was a little dumbfounded by it because I knew that my friend had not moved to Jamaica and I couldn't imagine who this letter was from. I opened the letter to read, "Your poem is so beautiful and inspiring! With my heart's infinite blessings, Guru."

I couldn't believe it...Guru had written to me!

❖ A confirmation of Guru's vision

Allow me to return to the very first interview that I had with Guru on his front porch. I remember as he meditated on me having the impression that he knew me. Recall also that I corrected Guru when he asked if my mother would mind my becoming a

The Early Days

student, saying, "No, my mother would *never* mind," but thinking to myself that perhaps my father might mind.

You see, my mother had really done most of the rearing of the family. My father was married to his pharmacy, although his loving influence was always present in our home and in my own life. My father would always joke that the key to my parents' success in marriage was that my mother recognized her proper place in the family. She would make the minor decisions, such as where we should live, where the kids should go to school or what kind of car we should drive, while she would "surrender" the truly important decisions to him—decisions such as "should we send a man to the moon?" or what our policy should be with regards to China!

At any rate, my mother had already experienced her two older sons going through their changes, which included getting into their share of teenage mischief. Jackie, my oldest brother, was straight out of the "American Graffiti" era and was definitely one of the tough guys. Lenny was Fabian (hair greased back and all!) reborn in a 1957 Chevy. Me, well, I was a full-blown hippie, drugs and all. (My youngest brother, Billy, didn't wait for his teenage years to create problems. He was a monster from birth, but turned out the best of the lot.)

Anyway, to demonstrate how she handled my mischief and why I was *sure* she wouldn't mind, when I was arrested for possession of marijuana (eventually everybody got arrested in those days), she came storming into the Scarsdale Police station absolutely irate...not at me...at the police! "How can you arrest my son? Why don't you get the real criminals? So what if he smokes a little marijuana, all the kids do!"

My mother was a short but large woman. When asked her height, she would describe herself as "5 by 5" and it was pretty accurate. And, because she was heavy, she was always hot. After bailing me out, she said quite deliberately in front of the police, "Sandy, next time you get arrested make sure it's an air-conditioned police station, or I'm not coming down to bail you out."

The Early Days

Such was my mother's tolerance and love, and so I presumed myself completely correct in assuring Guru that my mother would never mind, or so I thought. It actually struck me as somewhat humorous that he would ask.

When I first became a student, my early meditation life with Guru seemed to go pretty much unnoticed by my mother. I returned to Northwestern to complete my schooling, and after graduation came back and lived with my parents in Hartsdale, New York.

Once at home, my mother could not help but notice all the changes. My long hair and beard disappeared. I was getting up earlier. I would close my door whenever I was in my room. The occasional fragrance of incense would waft through the apartment.

Then one afternoon, while casually sitting at the kitchen table, seemingly out of nowhere, she inquired, "Sandy, what are you into now?" I explained that I had decided to study meditation and for three months I was going to study with an Indian spiritual Master.

You can imagine my shock and dismay when then and there she threatened, "If you are going to do that, I disown you and you'll have to move out of my house." I couldn't believe my ears. I had never heard words such as these coming from my mother! "I don't want you becoming a monk!" she screamed. I had no idea that she would have any concept of what this whole thing was about in the first place!

"I don't want to become a monk either!" I reassured her, and tried to convince her that it was just going to be for a few months, but my assurances were not enough. There was no appeasing her. She was true to her word. She disowned me so completely that indeed I had to move out of the house! Eventually she accepted me back, but there was always some resentment that I chose this lifestyle. She had wanted me to marry and have many grandchildren, and she was not happy at not having her wish fulfilled.

The Early Days

    This experience confirmed to me that in that first brief moment of meditation, Guru had seen something in my life that in my wildest dreams I had not anticipated. As it turned out, I was completely wrong about both my parents' responses, because my father became very receptive to the whole idea. In fact, as a result of my meditative life, my father and I rediscovered a closeness that we had lost during my hippie era, a closeness that I shall always cherish.

3

"Pop"

❖ A painful generation gap revisited

It is both difficult—and I must confess quite painful— to recall the separation that once existed between my father and me. I know it is not unusual for young men to experience a generation gap during their formative years, but this particular generation gap was enhanced by the social circumstances of the time. Viet Nam was being fought and witnessed in our living rooms, drugs were rampant, and an entire generation of young people rejected *en masse* the life-styles which their parents represented.

With incredible sweetness, I can recall moments I spent with my dad, "Pop" as I called him, when I was a young boy. On his way to work Saturday mornings, he would drop me off at White Plains Bowl so that I could play in the kid's league, and at 12 noon, he would pick me up to eat at Papa John's Italian Restaurant. I would order veal parmigiana with spaghetti, while my father would opt for the veal without the parmigiana. This was our

"Pop"

time. Afterwards, I would go with him to work at the pharmacy that was his life's work—Balter's Chemists in Elmsford, NY. I would work there all day and close the store with him. I would count the cash in the small register, while he closed out the main register.

My father had four sons, all well-loved by both parents, but I was my father's favorite. He held out the most hope for me as regards to doing something meaningful in life. Lenny, son number two, was mom's favorite. There was no jealousy between us boys, and we used our respective "favorite" status to our collective advantage. If we needed permission from mom for a particular thing, Lenny was the go-to guy. If pop's okay was required, the task fell to me. And so it was particularly hard for my father to witness me, his favorite son, walk down the road of drugged-out hippie.

Everyone used drugs in those days. It was part of the social climate. Selling drugs was just as commonplace as using them. On one occasion, I was talking with a friend on the phone about some drugs I had available to sell. Unbeknownst to me, my father was listening silently on another extension until he had heard enough. Suddenly he started screaming—and I mean *screaming*—at the top of his lungs. My father had already had two heart attacks, and I felt certain that he was going to have another right then and there. I had never seen him so upset. In hindsight, he was right to be so upset. So often, we as sons learn later in life that our fathers were actually right in the first place with their counsel.

Sadly, this experience was not enough to stop me from using drugs. I confess that I recall this incident with such sadness now, but it all worked out, thanks to Guru. While it was the drug overdose that ended my drug use, it was Guru who was responsible for my father and I finding each other again—and with a depth that I never dreamed possible.

Allow me to confess that tears of gratitude are welling up in my eyes for my father's love.

"Pop"

❖ My father's heart begins to melt

As I mentioned earlier, my becoming a student coincided with the end of my drug usage. While my mother regularly protested my spiritual life with Guru, my dad just watched, enjoyed and teased a bit. Of course, I had pictures of Guru, including the Transcendental, in my room. My father would lightheartedly ask that, since he had paid for my college education, couldn't I have at least one picture of him, you know, "just a small picture that could be put next to the Guru's?"

On another occasion, he attended a public meditation at Columbia University just to see what it was all about. As it so happened, while the first floor was full, the balcony of the auditorium was empty. Guru opened the evening by chanting "Aum" most soulfully. The next day or so, while I was meditating in my room, my father popped in with folded hands chanting, "Oyyyyyyyyyyy, there's nobody in the balcony. Oyyyyyyyyyyy!" This was his sense of humor.

❖ Sarama's house

And so it came that I moved out of my parents' home. It was okay. It was the right time for it. I had spent five years at college living on my own, creating my own space, and I no longer related to my father's apothecary jars which decorated the Balter household.

Since I had become close with Sarama as my mentor into Sri Chinmoy's path, she invited me to take a room in her home. Yoga at this time was experiencing a surge in popularity, and with that, interest in meditation was also peaking. As a result, Sarama was responsible for introducing many people to the path of Sri Chinmoy. I think that officially more than one hundred students came via Sarama. And I also think that it is to her credit that all the boys who lived in that house with her—Pulak, Rupantar, Sunil and myself—remained on the path all their lives.

So many wonderful memories are associated with that household. All the boys would get up to watch Guru early in the morn-

"Pop"

ing on television, as there was one station which opened its daily programming with Guru meditating. We were all awakened by Sunil who would exit his room early and blow his nose in the hallway. I can't speak for the others, but for me this sound suggested what it must have been like in the battlefield of Kurukshetra[1] when the conch shells were being blown. Sunil's nose-blowing shook the house. Rupantar would marvel at how I always had fresh candles on my shrine until he finally discovered they were plastic candles. All of us performed darkroom duty for Sarama and eventually became hatha yoga instructors.

    I, frankly, was not a great student, not that I am one now. But I had not completely found myself in Guru's path. I had strong attachments to my parents and little brother, and on Saturdays would prefer to see my brother playing football than to do "selfless service" like the others. This was obviously not lost on Guru. There would be special functions to which everyone from the house was invited except me.

❖ Chiropractic school or medical school

    At Northwestern, I majored in Biomedical Engineering as a conduit to medical school. In the year after graduation, I applied both to medical school and chiropractic school. I was accepted first at the National College of Chiropractic back in Chicago and I sent my letter of acceptance informing them that I would begin in September. Shortly thereafter I was accepted at Stony Brook Medical School in New York.

    There were many influences directing me to medical school. First, it was the more prestigious degree. At the time, there were no medical doctors on the path and I remember Sarama advising me, "The path could use a doctor." Second, the medical school was in New York, which meant I would still be able to see Guru

---

[1] In the Mahabharata, an immortal Indian epic, a great battle took place on the battlefield of Kurukshetra. The daily battles would begin with the blowing of conch shells.

with some regularity. Third, medicine was my own personal preference. Finally, there was the universal truth. What universal truth? There are many spiritual truths that all of history's great scriptures hold in common. Let me share with you a lesser-known truth which is nonetheless just as universal: any Jewish pharmacist wants a son to be a medical doctor. This truth is as concrete as any you'll encounter anywhere, and it was certainly true in the case of my own father.

On my behalf, Sarama asked Guru which profession I should pursue. Over the next three days, all I heard were various influences pointing to medical school. Medical school was gaining momentum emotionally. On the fourth day, I hadn't heard anything from Guru, so I assumed there would be no reply and sent off a letter of acceptance to medical school and a letter of rejection to the chiropractic school. This actually received Sarama's approval, so I felt pretty good about it. I also informed my father of my decision, which made him very happy and proud.

That night, Sarama returned from meditation and knocked on my door. I was just lying down to go to sleep. "Oh good, you're lying down," she said, knowing that was the best position for me to hear what she was about to say. "I spoke with Guru. He said you should go to chiropractic school. Knowing that you had just sent out your letter of acceptance to medical school, I started to say 'but Guru…' at which time Guru said, 'Fine. Let him do whatever he wants.'" Then she added, "I think Guru feels, though, you should really go to chiropractic school."

Guru's "let him do whatever he wants" most often meant one of two things: either "It is completely irrelevant to your spiritual life and any choice is perfectly fine," or, more likely, "Well, you're not going to listen to me anyway, so do whatever you want."

Oh God, now I had done it. I had already committed outwardly and inwardly to medical school, but I heard Guru's message as clearly as Sarama did. Over the next few days I had to muster up the courage to reverse my emotional momentum. I immediately called the chiropractic school and spoke to the dean of admis-

"Pop"

sions, explaining to him the situation that compelled me to originally reject chiropractic school, but that now I had changed my mind and hoped it was not too late. He told me he was just reading my letter when I called and was only too happy to accept someone who was rejecting medical school for chiropractic school. "I'll tear up your letter," he said.

Then there was my father. I called him up and said, "Dad, I want to take you out to dinner."

"What's the occasion?" he asked.

"I'll tell you when we get there. I'll meet you at Papa John's, my treat." Yes, the same Papa John's where my father and I would eat lunch after my childhood bowling league!

We met that evening and after we ate I said, "Dad, I don't want to disappoint you at all, but I want you to know that I have decided to go to chiropractic school instead of medical school." I did not tell him that Guru was the one who influenced me to make this decision, but rather chose to say that chiropractic was more natural and more in tune with my life style, yadda, yadda, yadda.

I was really impressed with my dad's response. While he did try to convince me to go to medical school, once he had made his case, in no way did he impose his will, which would have made it more difficult for me. Instead, he let me know that if this was my decision, so be it, and he would be happy for me.

While this whole thing may appear insignificant, in fact, it was just the opposite. I sensed my father was freeing me from the nest. And, from that point on, our relationship changed, growing more intimate day by day.

Much more significantly, here was an important crossroads (so it seemed) in my life, and I chose to listen to Guru's counsel, which I felt was based on something deeper, instead of heeding the advice of all the other outer influences.

In practical terms, it was the most important decision I made in my early studentship. It entailed leaving New York, which meant moving away from my parents and old friends, the two things keeping me from becoming a better student. When I moved back to Chicago, I knew I had to either make the grade inwardly, or fall by the wayside. I took my meditation much more seriously. I went with the idea of starting a Sri Chinmoy Centre in Chicago, which meant starting to give talks and I did so with Guru's blessings. Little did I know then that giving talks would end up playing such a large role in my spiritual life.

When I walked into the chiropractic school for the very first time, I had an immediate impression that I would only be doing this for a few years. Indeed, that was the case.

After practicing for two years or so, I couldn't help noticing that after treating a patient, I would walk out of the treatment room with that patient's symptoms. They felt better, while I felt worse. This was not a comfortable experience for me, and I suspected that it was unhealthy for my spiritual life. By this time, I had actually started working on Guru's leg pain, so at the appropriate time I told him of my experience and asked him if I could stop practicing. "What would you do?" he replied. "How about a restaurant?" I suggested. (What was I thinking?) "Fine. Do it, do it," came his reply.

A few years later, I had the opportunity to bring a final close to this chapter on medical school versus chiropractic school. I suspected that Guru's original counsel had nothing to do with which healing modality was better, but rather had everything to do with getting me out of New York, where there would be some hope of my succeeding on our path.

"Guru," I asked, "when you told me to go to chiropractic school way back when, did you even know what a chiropractor was, or was there something else at play?"

"It all served its purpose," he smiled. "It all served its purpose."

❖ Tumors don't read textbooks

In late 1973, shortly after I began chiropractic school, the cause of my mother's recurring migraines was discovered. My mother was diagnosed with a meningioma–a brain tumor. While this kind of tumor was classically benign, it still required brain

"Pop"

surgery. In those days, brain surgery literally required the skull to be sawed open and removed so that the brain could be accessed. My mother was a vivacious, optimistic woman, and she chose to attack this operation with courage and certainty. Indeed, her surgery was a complete success. She came out of it with flying colors.

While she was recovering, my father and I visited the surgeon's office for post-operative consultation. As fate would have it, the pathologist's report was on the doctor's desk and I asked to read it. The doctor informed us that, based on the size of the tumor, it probably had been growing for 20 years. He added that the tumor was totally removed and should not return, and if it did, it would take another 20 years. My dad was relieved, needless to say, but I wasn't. You see, I noted in the pathologist's report one phrase, "some atypical mitoses noted". Atypical mitoses is a cardinal sign of malignancy, and I questioned the doctor about it. "Oh," he said, "tumors don't read textbooks. This tumor is benign. There's nothing to worry about."

❖ **A generation gap dissolved...and then some!**
From the time I became Guru's student, my father and I had regular discussions about my spiritual life. While I was in chiropractic school in Chicago, we would speak at great length on the phone. He would ask questions or commiserate. On one occasion, he told *his* older brother, my uncle Bill, to speak with me, because my dad felt meditation might help him. It's a little funny counseling your own uncle as to how he might change his life! On another occasion, I remember my father admitting, "If I were your age, I would do exactly what you are doing right now." There were times I actually felt like I was his father.

❖ **"I'm so glad you're home"**
A year and a half after my mother's first surgery, I received a call from my dad. "Something's wrong. I think it's possible that

"Pop"

the tumor is back." He went on to list the symptoms which ranged from "she left the turkey in the oven until the meat fell off" to "she's sleeping 18 hours a day". I told dad to take her to the doctor and see.

Upon seeing the same doctor who performed the original brain surgery, my mother declared, "They're not going in my head again." Unfortunately, there was no choice. The tumor–the benign tumor–had returned, larger than before. My mother, for obvious reasons, did not have the same resolve regarding a second surgery. She understood the implications.

The surgery lasted seven hours, ending with the doctor admitting, "We did the best we could, but we couldn't get it all." My mother returned home, not quite the same. It was only six months later when I received a phone call I will never forget. When I answered the phone, I heard only two words. "It's back." My father's voice was quivering with angst and uncertainty. I had never heard him like that.

"What's back?" I asked.

"The tumor, it's back. I don't know what to do."

"Dad, I will call you right back." I got off the phone and immediately called my older brother Lenny and explained to him that I had never heard dad sound like that. I asked him to call dad and if he sensed the same thing, I would fly home from Chicago immediately. A few minutes later, Lenny called me back. "Go home," he said.

I made a flight reservation and took a flight to New York without even having time to call my father. I got home to our Hartsdale apartment at 1 a.m. and left my bags in the foyer by the front door. Then I quietly snuck into the bed that was still reserved for me whenever I returned home.

The next morning I was awakened by my father. He was clasping my hand, rocking gently while simply repeating, "I'm so glad you're home, I'm so glad you're home..."

"I'm glad I'm home too, dad. Now we'll do all that needs to be done together."

"Pop"

Over the next three days, my dad and I talked and talked and talked. We talked about life, death, Guru and God. My father told me stories of his own childhood. I am sure I heard things none of my brothers ever heard. Guru was in the midst of it all, because this could never have happened without his influence on my life. I told my father that despite the fact that he felt that my mother's situation was hopeless, still she had to go for the third surgery. I told him that he would never be able to live with himself if he thought that he had not done everything possible. He agreed.

At her bedside just before the surgery, I had the premonition that my mother would never come home again. She never did. Post-surgical care required the attention only a nursing home could give. And while she seemed to recede into what appeared to be a surgically induced lobotomy, I always felt it was something different—I felt she was depressed at witnessing her own condition. Why did I feel that? Because she would always perk up when someone new walked into the room, would still laugh at a joke, but then recede into silence again.

Once, I was alone with her. She greeted me with a few words and then her usual silent absent gaze. She didn't speak. I felt compelled to ask, "Mom, if I could do anything for you right now, anything at all, what would you have me do?" My mother broke her silence, "You know exactly what I want. You know exactly what I want." I did. I knew she wanted to leave.

From that point on, my prayers for her changed. Whatever was to be her destiny, whatever God wanted for her, whether it be to heal or to pass, let it happen quickly. My mother died August 25, 1976.

During this entire experience, my father and I continually traded roles as father and son. Guru's role in all this was not lost on my father. He told me, "I am so grateful for what Guru has done for us." He told me that he wanted to meet Guru, but sadly that never happened. And of course, upon my father's passing, Guru took special care of my father, but that is another story.

"Pop"

❖ **September 1, 1976–receiving my name**

I remember the date I received my name, because two significant things happened the week before. As I mentioned, my mother passed away just a few days earlier on August 25. I actually attended her funeral on the morning of Guru's birthday, and then left later that afternoon for Guru's Birthday Celebration. The second event was, in fact, a process. Guru was "lightening the boat." Many local students had stopped aspiring and, for the sake of those who were trying to aspire, Guru felt the necessity to ask these folks to leave the path. This was a very painful thing for Guru, but he felt it was necessary.

I had requested an interview with Guru to discuss some things to do with the Midwest Centres. Back then there were four or five Centres in the Midwest. On the morning of September 1st, we were all at the Jamaica High School sports field. Guru called me over to him. "Good boy, good boy, I wanted to give you an interview but, because of this thing (having to ask students to leave), it is hurting me so much, please forgive me, but I can't give it to you now. Tonight, please come to my house at 7:30 p.m. I'm going to give you your name."

That evening, along with some 7-10 other people, I received my spiritual name. On our spiritual path, one did not receive a name as a matter of initiation at a set time. For each person it was different. Guru would give a name to a student when the inner personality clearly began to emerge. The name reflects that personality, and as such, receiving one's name is a real blessing-boon in that it enables the seeker to identify with their innermost qualities.

There has always been a ritual of sorts attached to receiving one's name, and over time that ritual has changed. To me, and I am sure that I speak for others, it is a very sacred thing. That evening, Guru called each of us forward one at a time.

When my turn arrived, after meditating some time on me, Guru placed his palm on the crown of my head and, from a very high meditation, mantricly said,

"Pop"

> *"You are bringing to the fore your soul's capacity and your heart's capacity. For that, I am extremely delighted, extremely proud of you. With my heart's deepest joy and delight, I am giving you your soul's name.*
>
> *Pradhan, Pradhan, Pradhan.*
>
> *It is a very powerful Sanskrit name...descended from the Vedic era. Great, one who is great inwardly on the strength of his heart's openness to the light, to the truth, to the supreme reality. Great. Your soul's greatness is being manifested through its conscious, fully awakened and constant openness to the way of the Beloved Supreme. So greatness is an openness. Greatness in your dedication, in your oneness with your soul for the manifestation of the Absolute Truth.*
>
> *P-R-A-D-H-A-N, P-R-A-D-H-A-N*
>
> *Pradhan, Pradhan"*

It is a beautiful name and I am humbled to have received such a name. Some day I hope to fulfill my Guru's vision.

❖ Receiving my pink slip

The following year, Guru said that unfortunately he would have to apply the same process of lightening the boat to the Centres outside the local area. Certainly, I could be one of those to leave. Day in, day out, I do so many things wrong.

It was late October. I arrived home late in the evening after giving some talks on meditation in Milwaukee. Upon returning home, I opened my mailbox to find a telegram. The telegram had Guru's return address on it.

"Uh oh," I thought. I knew what this letter had to be. At long last, Guru had come to my name on the list of those who unfortunately he had to ask to leave. I quickly ascended the steps that led to my bedroom, closed the door behind me, sat down at my meditation area and prayed for a moment to get up the courage to open the envelope. Finally, with a sense of impending doom,

I opened the telegram to read:

> "Dearest Pradhan,
>   Infinite Love, Blessings, Concern, Pride and Gratitude
>   on your birthday.
>   Your Guru."

From the depths to the heights in six seconds flat!

4

My Father's Passing

❖ I am your Eternity's father

When my father passed away, it was not completely unexpected. He had already experienced five heart attacks and two bouts of congestive heart failure. It was March 17, 1978 at around 10 a.m., when my younger brother called me from New York with the news. I immediately made two phone calls. The first call was to my dear friend, Ashrita, whose responsibility was message-giver to and from Guru. I told Ashrita about my father's passing, and asked him to inform Guru. The second call was to make a flight reservation. To my surprise, within an hour or so, I received a call back from Ashrita. He informed me that Guru said upon my arrival in New York, I should come to his home, and to please bring a photo of my father. Guru added that I could come anytime until 2 a.m. (Guru used a photo as a tool to access "the soul" of that individual. We, as seekers, will often speak of the soul as a theoretical concept, but for genuine spiritual Masters, the soul is absolutely real. Guru often said that he could see the soul as "more real" or "more clearly" than our physical.)

My father's passing occurred at a time in my life when I felt a little shaky, spiritually speaking. I was just opening my chiropractic office and spending a lot of money in the process. Perhaps my meditation time was sacrificed a bit as all this was happening. The net effect was that I wasn't feeling particularly good about myself spiritually.

As a result of this, I was not exactly prepared to stand in front of Guru. I must add that this is a completely wrong attitude. I've learned this since. There is perhaps no more important time to stand in front of your spiritual Teacher as when you are feeling least worthy. But that was not my wisdom at the time of this significant occurrence.

My flight arrived late in the evening, around 11 p.m. I made my way to Hartsdale where my brother lived with my father, showered and drove down to Guru's home in Jamaica, N.Y. It was 1 a.m. when I finally found myself standing on the street in front of Guru's home. The lights were off for the most part.

I stood there for a few minutes with a photo of my father affectionately surrounded by his four sons. It was clear which one was my father, both from an age standpoint and also from a focal standpoint. He was clearly the source of all the family vanity.

At this point, all my insecurity came forward. I knew I wasn't in a particularly good consciousness. I thought to myself, "Gee, the lights are out. Maybe I should go home, get in a decent morning meditation and then come back." This way, I could tell Guru that I was actually there but, because the lights were out, I didn't want to bother him. Very fortunately, my stupidity was corrected by another thought, "Your father has passed away. For God's sake, this is for him, not for you!"

I gathered my courage and went to the side door and knocked very gently, and I mean very, very gently. I thought that if no one answered, I could definitely go home and be able to tell Guru the next day, "I even knocked!" There was no answer.

My Father's Passing

If I knocked a second time with no answer, I would be fully justified in leaving. I knocked again, this time a bit harder. With that, the light came on, the door at the top of the stairs opened, and I could see Guru looking out at me.

I could hear him as he descended the steps, "Oh, I am so sorry good boy, so sorry." Then as he opened the door, he asked, "Did you bring a picture?"

This is the picture I showed to Guru. The Balter Boys: My dad, in the center, with my older brothers Lenny and Jack standing behind him, and my little brother Billy kneeling on the right. I'm kneeling on the left.

"Yes, Guru," I said as I handed him the picture, feeling it needed no further explanation, as anyone would know which of the five men was my father.

I was so surprised when Guru asked, "Which one is it?"

I shrugged off my surprise and simply pointed to the man in the center of the photo. "This one," I clarified.

My Father's Passing

"Which one?" again Guru asked.
"This one," I said with a bit more emphasis.
"Which one?"
"This one!"
"Which one?"
"This one!!"
"Which one?"

At this point, I no longer understood why it wasn't obvious. Then the thought occurred to me that perhaps Guru had received a message that my brother had died and this was the source of his confusion. With that, I finally clarified it.

"This one, Guru. That's my father!"

At long last, it became all clear. With his eyes closed, soulfully, lovingly and softly, Guru repeated over and over, "I am your Eternity's father. I am your Eternity's father. I am your Eternity's father. I am your Eternity's father. I am your Eternity's father." Perhaps twenty times he said it and, with each utterance, all my inner insecurity-angst dissipated to be replaced with my Guru's unvanquishable love. Then he opened his eyes and said, "I will do everything for your father that I can."

As I was leaving, he put the porch lights on and waved and smiled at me most compassionately and lovingly. It was a smile I will never forget.

❖ Two fathers

I am always fond of saying that I have two fathers: Irving (along with Mom Beatrice) who parented Sandy, and Guru who gave birth to Pradhan. Well, the day after my father's passing and the late-night encounter with Guru, I received a message at my home, this time from Savyasachi, one of Guru's main assistants. "Guru said your father was extremely receptive and that he wants to hold a special meditation for your father tomorrow night."

I was surprised and delighted. Both my older brother Lenny and I attended this special meditation. It was an unusual meditation, to say the least. Guru called me up and had me sit in front of him. He told me to sit as close as possible and he asked me to remove my glasses! And then he meditated most powerfully. At a certain point, he placed his hand on my head and with his thumb massaged my third eye. (That point located between the eyebrows, a little above, is referred to as the "third eye." It is a spiritual center for inner vision.) It was a most unique meditation and experience.

Guru's most sacred blessing at the special meditation he held for my father.

Afterwards, he commented, "Sandy's father's soul was sitting right next to him, most devoted, most soulfully. He was playing a musical instrument most effusively. I don't know if he played any instrument in this lifetime, but here he was definitely playing with utmost devotion." (Again, recall my earlier comment that for Guru, the soul is absolutely real, accessible and visible.)

My Father's Passing

I was struck by two things. One was the word "effusively." I could only imagine what that meant, having never heard it before. The second was this—I had been Pradhan for two years or so at this point. Yet when Guru referred to my earthly dad, he said "Sandy's father..."

I am grateful for both of my fathers.

❖ Your father was here

I can always invoke a sense of my father. During the time subsequent to my mother's passing, as I mentioned earlier, he and I grew closer than the closest. It's hard to imagine any father and son being more inwardly close than we were.

A few years following my father's passing, I was on Guru's porch with about 30 other students. It was my birthday, although nothing was said about celebrating it. Finally, as the last event of the evening, a birthday cake was brought out and handed to Guru, and Guru started to speak. I folded my hands *assuming* it was my birthday cake (which it was), but I began to doubt it when I heard what Guru was saying.

Although I can't remember his precise words, I do remember that the words were so flattering that I began to doubt that the birthday cake was for me. In fact, at a certain point, very slyly, I looked around to see if anyone else was sitting nearby with their hands expectantly folded as if it were their birthday! Whatever words Guru was saying were so flattering they couldn't possibly belong to me. It wasn't until Guru started singing "Happy Birthday" and I heard my name that I was convinced.

Wow!

Anyway, afterwards the conversation with Guru became casual. "Do you remember when I gave you your first interview on this porch?"

"Yes, Guru."

"You do? Okay, what color pants were you wearing?"

I shrugged.

"Green!" he said, "and you were carrying something in your hand."

I started telling stories about the early days with my parents and how they reacted differently—how my mother temporarily disowned me and how my father became quite receptive.

"Yes, your father was quite receptive," Guru affirmed with a look that made me suspicious.

I inquired about my father, "Guru, does my father's soul ever appear before you? I mean, does he ever come to you?"

There was a moment's pause and then with a sheepish grin on his face, he explained, "Why do you think I said all these nice things in front of you? Because he was here! Inwardly, I could have communicated it with your soul and his soul, but because it made him feel a little proud to see his son flattered in front of all these other people, I said these things out loud!"

5

At the Feet of my Master

Many of these stories come from a special role with which I have been blessed. I, along with three or four other "doctorish" boys, worked on Guru's legs in an attempt to resolve his never-ending leg pain. Guru's legs seemed to bear the brunt of his duties as spiritual Teacher, and they were in constant pain.

Please understand that the position of sitting at the Master's feet is a time-honored, sacred position and opportunity and, as a result, the boys who performed this task were often perceived by others as being special in some way.

Forgive me, but my perspective is different. Blessed, yes– special, no. I simply had the remarkably good fortune to be given this role by Sri Chinmoy. He could easily have chosen someone else.

I do know one thing. I can never be grateful enough for this special opportunity that was presented to me. I simply do not know how.

❖ NOAMS: No Outer Attention Misery Syndrome
(Note: This is a story which could rightly be placed under the section on scoldings, but because it is a lesson intimately linked to massaging Guru, I have placed it here.)

This is a story which has many lessons and experiences associated with it. One thing I've learned over the years is that God does not have time to waste time with my life. Every moment has its purpose. I, on the other hand, have an uncanny capacity to waste my time, or so it seems. But God uses even my worst moments to His best advantage! The story that follows and the lessons that came with it were years in the making.

When I first became a student, I felt there was no necessity to speak with Guru, and therefore never sought to do so. For five years, I never initiated a word with Guru, even though I was the leader of one of his Centres. Sometimes he would pass by and say, "You are all right?" or something like that, but it was rarely more than that.

One year, during a Christmas trip in Bermuda, I was talking with a friend of mine who was also the leader of another Midwest Centre. He told me that every time he visited New York to see Guru, he requested an interview and got it. This, frankly, awoke the jealousy-flame in me, so I decided I would ask for an interview, and to my surprise and joy I received it! (In the early days when students were fewer, interviews were more commonplace. Later, because Guru was responsible for so many students, interviews became a rarity, and frankly weren't as necessary as we students might think! Our inner faith and meditation often did the trick, and certainly Guru encouraged us to cultivate and rely on this inner form of interview.)

This was the very dawn of an outer relationship with Guru that twisted, turned, and became richer and more purposeful over the years. Many brother and sister students admired those who would appear to have a closer outer role with Guru than they might have had. That role would *only* be there if it were necessary for the progress of the student. It is not any indication of the Master's affection for the student. He is not bound by such things.

As a student of more than thirty-nine years, I have witnessed that Guru gave you just what you needed at just the right time. If it served your aspiration-progress to have an outer relationship with you, Guru would carve one out, and he did so at the appropriate time. However, some students are better suited to a purely inner relationship, and that is precisely what Guru cultivated. (Please see the section called "Appearances" on page 51 for an interesting side-effect of NOAMS!)

Parallel to this, it has also been my observation that rarely does the student ever get what he thinks that he needs, deserves or wants. When someone else gets attention and you don't, you feel miserable. Even if you get outer attention, you want more. And sometimes you get outer attention when you don't want it. All of these experiences are symptoms of a common syndrome. I call this syndrome, "No Outer Attention Misery Syndrome," or NOAMS, for short.

But back to my story. Some twenty-five years ago, as a result of a bad fall, Guru injured his back and developed a severe sciatica down his left leg. He also subsequently developed a "foot slap" on his right side which became apparent whenever he ran, a fitness activity he loved to do. When he placed his right foot down, it would quickly drop, making a slapping noise as it did so. Guru was regularly receiving various kinds of treatement and leg massage to try to relieve it.

I was a chiropractor, and in casual conversation I mentioned to Savyasachi that I thought chiropractic treatments might fix Guru's problem. I want to emphasize that I was not at all seeking to do it. Neither did I feel qualified nor spiritually pure enough to work on Guru. Well, apparently Savyasachi mentioned my suggestion to Guru, because the next morning, in front of a number of students, and in a very public place, I was shocked when Guru

At the Feet of my Master

called me forward to treat him chiropractically, and then work and massage his painful legs. I was surprised and nervous.

This moment was the beginning of a different and more obvious outer relationship with Guru. Soon I became Guru's main visiting masseur, and with this new role came an entire new set of experiences. You see, before this time I was pretty much an unknown, an obscure ex-New York student now living in Chicago. Now I was suddenly thrust front and center, massaging my spiritual Teacher. Not only did my relationship with Guru suddenly change, but my relationship with everyone else did too. There is a reason for this. As I mentioned earlier, from an historical perspective, occupying the seat at your Teacher's feet is a time-honored and most sacred position. Suddenly, the person known as Pradhan garnered a new respect from his student family.

Everybody looked at me differently. In fact, even my fellow Chicago students were affected by it. Once, a Canadian student approached a young girl in our Centre, "What's it like to work with him?"

"With who?" she responded.

"You know, with him, Pradhan?"

The girl was dumbfounded (rightfully so) and said, "I dunno...he tells a lot of jokes?" She was searching for an answer and couldn't quite figure out why she was being asked.

Much more importantly (and inappropriately), the dreaded disease started. I came to use this role as a gauge for Guru's affection for me. As long as I was at Guru's feet, I was okay. If not, something was wrong—clearly Guru was upset with me. As a result of all this, a not so subtle pride-attachment developed. Yes, I became very attached to the role.

Every year at Christmas time, Sri Chinmoy traveled to some part of the world with a group of students. Well, one Christmas took us to Japan. There Guru had me accompany him everywhere he went. I was carrying his bags, reserving seats and massaging him at every opportunity. I was in outer-attention-bliss syndrome. (This is a close relation to NOAMS, but is much more delusional.)

The following year, our Christmas trip brought us to Venezuela, and I was looking forward to playing the same role. I was in for a surprise. Guru did not speak to me. Not one word. And with that, day by day, I was becoming more miserable. Of course, no one knew this. I dared not share it with anybody out of embarrassment. Nevertheless, it was there with me, growing deeper and deeper every day.

There were three or four boys who played this role on the trip. I remember one fateful evening Guru called out for Nirvik, another masseur. Now, I knew that none of these boys was around, so I quickly yelled out, "He's not here, Guru!"

"Not here? All right, is Savyasachi here then?"

"He's not here either, Guru," came my voice.

One by one, Guru called for other boys to work on his leg, and over and over my voice was heard, "He's not here."

Finally, there was just me left. I waited. And waited. After a thoughtful pause Guru said, "All right, since there is no one here to massage my leg, let's go downstairs to the other room."

Ugh. I was in agony, devastated. Clearly I had fallen and I was in the abyss. Everyone went downstairs except for me. I remained upstairs with my head in my hands. A few moments later I heard someone's voice. It was one of the girls who regularly cook for Guru. She told me, "Guru said you should bring down his chair."

"He did!?" and I did just that. Little did I know that this was an omen of what was to come.

Days passed and still I was not called by Guru. My misery quietly and privately grew with each day.

It was now New Year's Eve, and Guru held a beautiful meditation under a clear moon on the veranda outside the hotel. Afterwards, he gave a significant talk while Nirvik worked on his leg, and then Guru asked for questions. Ashrita was the first to raise his hand and ask a question which Guru answered. Then the moment came—I asked a question. Well, Guru did not answer my question. Instead, with a very serious tone, I was greeted with, "Good boy, what you need is an entirely new attitude towards your spiritual life."

From the seriousness of Guru's tone, I knew this was the big one. I immediately began shrinking inwardly and tried to shrink outwardly. He continued, "Here you are suffering so much. You're so miserable because Nirvik is massaging me and I haven't asked you to massage me. You think that I don't care for you, that I don't love you. Everything is demand, demand, demand."

He went on. "You have to feel at every moment that I know what is best for you and at every moment that I love you. If today I smile at you, you have to feel 'Today Guru is showing his love for me by smiling at me,' and tomorrow if I don't smile at you, you should feel 'My Guru is showing his love for me by not smiling at me.'"

This is the condensed version of Guru's response but it captures the essence. Now you have to remember that this message was being powerfully reinforced by the fact that inwardly Guru had been perfectly reading my inner misery. Without my telling him, he clearly saw my attachment-suffering, so I was easily convinced that even without the outer communication, he knew what was happening in my life.

Guru wasn't finished. It went on to be a general talk to everybody about selflessness and about demanding. This was the start of a number of messages given to all of us, spanning a period of years, about selfless giving without any expectation of return.

Anyway, it was a serious scolding. It was the kind of scolding that brought students over to me saying things like, "You know, if you weren't so strong, Guru wouldn't have done that publicly," as they patted me on the back. Someone actually sent flowers to my room anonymously!

When Guru gives anyone a talk like this, it is a great motivator for intense introspection and change. I didn't leave my room for the next three days and spent that time analyzing Guru's words which remain indelibly printed on my heart. I prayed. I meditated. I discovered that, indeed, Guru was right—more than right. I saw that there was not a single action that I did without some expectation for an acknowledgment—a smile, a thank you or whatever. (And not only with Guru, but with everyone.) It was then that I made a promise. I was determined to become a "utility" student; that I would be happy no matter what; that I would never doubt Guru's love for me; and that selflessness would become a theme for my life.

Well, Guru has an aphorism, "God has made my realisation easy. How I wish Him to make my nature's transformation easy also." It was easy to see the task at hand. It was easy to make a commitment to change. In fact, it was *not* easy to let go of my pride-attachment to that role.

When we returned home, Guru put me back on the massage role. The following year during the April Celebrations, Guru called me over to him. He told me that because I had been working hard, I should just relax during this celebration. Guru was being nice to me, but I was still not prepared for him not talking to me or not calling on me to work on him.

About a week into the celebration, I was in the throes of NOAMS when I walked into Lucille's Diner, a favorite local eatery in Queens. Ashrita happened to be there sitting at the counter with his head leaning a little sadly in his hand. I sat next to him and assumed the exact same position. Besides owning the most Guinness world records, Ashrita Furman, as I mentioned earlier, is Guru's main message-giver and probably spoke to Guru two to three times a day

Anyway, we were both sitting at the counter, a little mopey, heads leaning on our hands, when I turned to Ashrita and asked, "Ashrita, is Guru upset with me? He hasn't spoken to me this entire celebration."

Ashrita assured me with his typical enthusiasm, "Nah, are you kidding? No way!"

"Are you sure?" I asked, and he reassured me. There was silence again.

A few moments of silence passed and Ashrita turned to me and asked, "Pradhan, is Guru upset with me? He hasn't spoken to me either!"

And I assured him with the same enthusiasm he showed me only a minute before, "Of course not!"

Of course, a moment later we looked at each other and started to laugh. Here we were both suffering from the same disease, the classic NOAMS. Realizing this, I recommitted to becoming that utility student.

Well, the process took years. Every time I saw Guru, I would do so with the anticipation of massaging him. And every time I wasn't asked, I would feel a little jealous, insecure and unhappy that someone else was performing the task. But I was fighting that feeling, so it bothered me a little less and less each time it happened.

A real resolution did not come until our visit to Thailand many years later. We were in the city of Chiang Mai, meeting in a room provided by a hotel different from where we were actually staying. I had been in a pretty good consciousness and felt that I had earned a trip to Guru's feet. Then it happened. Guru asked a brand new person to work on his legs. I was quite tired, and when I'm tired the wrong forces have an easy go of it, and they attacked me without mercy. I became upset and close to angry! Recognizing this pattern for what it was, I left the meeting room for my hotel room and decided it best to sleep it off.

Fortunately, when I awoke, I did so with some inspiration. I remembered my promise to be unconditional. I decided that I had to know what it was to love God selflessly, and so I sat down to meditate with the full determination to stay there until I could feel an iota of selfless love for God.

It didn't take long before I discovered that I had no idea how to love God unconditionally—absolutely no idea. I had only one recourse. I invited, I begged, I pleaded for God to enter into me to show me how to love Him selflessly. I don't know what happened or how, whether it was imagined or real, but I felt God enter into me with an overwhelming love. That's all that there was—an emanation of love. With that, suddenly and clearly I heard a distinct message in Guru's voice saying, "Why do you want to settle for my feet when I want to give you my heart?" A smile came to my face that was so broad it almost ached.

I cannot say how long I was there, but after some time I was inspired to go back to the meeting place. When I walked in, Guru was just preparing to leave. Everyone was standing, anticipating Guru's departure. Guru was still seated and reached for a few last cashews as he was about to rise from his chair. He glanced up at me for just a moment as I arrived. He asked, "Oh Pradhan, why are you smiling?" He did not look at me again.

"I'm smiling because..." I hesitated a moment.

Guru repeated without looking, "Yes, why are you smiling?"

"I'm smiling because I know that you love me." Both the boys and girls let out a collective "ooh" but they were of distinctively different tones—the boys a bit mocking, the girls more empathetic.

"I love you?" he asked, still not looking at me, still casually noshing on cashews.

"Yes," I affirmed. "You love me."

Without ever looking up at me, and ever so firmly he said, "Fine. I love you. Now, remember this for Eternity."

With that, I was released from my attachment. May I be blessed to remember this message forever.

❖ Appearances

One of the cardinal symptoms of NOAMS is that you find yourself wishing you were getting what somewhat else is getting. What you get is never enough. This phenomenon is humorously and perfectly exemplified in an experience I had a dear friend as Guru was walking by the two of us.

As it happened, I had just arrived in New York and was standing in the hallway next to a my friend as Guru was leaving the meeting. When he saw me, he acknowledged me by giving me a "ho-o." This was a somewhat neutral greeting, not the overly exuberant "ho-o-oo-o" that comes with a joyful elevation in tone, or its opposite, "oy." It was just neutral, or so it seemed to me.

When Guru had walked a little past us, with hands still folded, out of my side of the mouth I asked my friend, "Was that good or bad?"

"It was good, definitely good," he said.

"Are you sure?"

"Well, let's put it this way—I wish he had done it to me."

"That's funny," came my final reply. "I wish he had done it to you too!"

We both laughed.

I can certainly understand how an observer might conclude that someone "massaging the Master" must be in some way, well, for lack of a better term, "special," or perhaps, especially close to the Master. My response to that is, "Joke." As I said earlier, as far as I am concerned, I happened to be a piece of fruit picked for this particular task. The role itself is of the highest honor, but that does not in and of itself elevate the person performing the task.

And, because of the weight we tend to place on outer appearances, there is often a difference between those appearances and the inner reality.

❖ "So Ron has left"

For a number of years, I shared massage duties with a local New York disciple. He was a medical doctor. The two of us were always linked. We were both doctors, both Jewish, both spectacled. I roomed with him for a number of years. He would massage Guru full time, but when I visited, the duty generally would fall to me.

When I say that he massaged Guru full time, I mean full time. This young man found himself near Guru for hours a day and was considered one of Guru's closest students. In fact, Guru would often publicly praise him for his dedication and aspiration.

As I mentioned, when I came to New York I roomed with this friend. However, one time when a visit was pending, I called him to tell him I was coming and he asked me to find someplace else to stay. Not only was I surprised to hear this request, but I was very uncomfortable with the tone of it. Something felt terribly wrong, and I decided to call Ashrita to inform him that I was concerned about my friend.

Upon hearing my comment, Ashrita told me, "Well, Guru must know. He's with Guru all the time."

"I know. I'm just doing my duty." Guru asks us to inform him if we feel someone is not doing well.

Ashrita acquiesced and said he would mention my concern to Guru. Whether he in fact did or not, I don't actually know.

As fate would have it, a few months later this particular boy left the path. The evening of his departure, Guru called me to work on his leg.

"So, Ron has left," he said.

"Yes, I heard." I continued, "You know, Guru, for the last three months I have been quite concerned about him."

"What three months?" Guru replied. "For the last three years he has been struggling. I have been giving him all this attention for the last few years to save his spiritual life. Not only has he left, but his soul has severed all ties with me."

This perplexed me. "Guru, how can that be? How can someone spend years massaging you and be at your side, yet the soul severs ties with you?"

"The soul severs ties with me so as to deprive the mind and vital of any real and deep inner joy. On the one hand, it is a kind of punishment...the soul is extremely angry with the other members of the inner family. On the other hand, this feeling of loss may be the only thing which re-awakens him to his own inner reality."

So you see, here is a case where by every measure an individual appears to be close to the Master, yet in reality, something else is happening.

And certainly, I am not above this "delusion of appearance".

At the Feet of my Master

❖ **"I am leaving the Centre"**

Around 1988 or so, I was going through a particularly difficult time in the Centre. The first Victory's Banner Restaurant had closed, which I took as a personal failure. I was financially in bad shape, and my relationship with some of the other Chicago students had soured to total ugly discomfort. I was very unhappy, and reached a point where I just couldn't cope with the Centre anymore. A concert was scheduled for Cincinnati, and all the Chicago students were journeying to Ohio, leaving Chicago empty. I saw this as an opportunity to pack my bags and depart.

I want to clarify that I did not want to leave Guru, only the Centre itself, essentially to be left to my own life with Guru and have no one else to answer to, or be responsible for. I wrote a letter to Guru informing him as such and faxed it to Ashrita to present to Guru. It was terribly painful and even more so when I called Ashrita to inform him of my decision and to expect a fax from me. He told me he would inform Guru right away.

True to his word, at the first opportunity Ashrita approached Guru with my letter saying it was urgent. Guru asked what it was about. Ashrita told him of my intention to leave. Guru responded, "Leave the Centre, or leave the path?"

Ashrita had to call me to get some clarification on this. He confessed he was surprised by the question. I told him that I knew what Guru meant. I did not want to leave him. I only wanted to leave the Centre situation because it had become so painful.

A few minutes later, Ashrita called. "Guru is asking you to please come to Cincinnati so that he can say goodbye to you, and bless you one more time before you leave." I could not say no, although it disrupted my plans to pack and leave while everyone was driving to Cincinnati. As far as they knew, I was not going. Instead of driving with them, I flew in order to keep my distance, and arranged for a single room in Guru's hotel.

I arrived and checked in hours before Guru's plane was due to land. Shortly, I received a call from the airplane. It was Ashrita again. "Guru said you will drive him while in Cincinnati."

"Okay," I acquiesced, and rented a car so I could pick Guru up at the airport.

All this time, no one else save for Ashrita knew what was taking place. The time came to pick Guru up and I waited at the pick-up area of the airport while students escorted Guru at his arrival. Guru was greeted by the husband-wife team who served as Centre leaders and had arranged for the concert. They opened the car door for Guru who entered and smiled broadly at me. I thought Guru would have me alone in the car, so I was surprised when Guru told the two Centre leaders to get in the back seat.

I was not alone with Guru until we reached the hotel when our hosts left Guru and his overnight luggage alone with me in the elevator. Guru turned to me and very sweetly said, "I see you have already left me. It is all right. You have been in my boat for so many years, I can easily be in your boat for a few years."

Tears began to well up in my eyes. Then he added, "On the other hand, I think if you left me today, tomorrow your heart will be crying and crying and crying."

That was it. I burst into tears. "I don't know what's happening to me," I confessed. "I don't know what could bring me to write you that letter."

"These forces come to the fore just to be illumined," Guru said. There was more to his loving guidance but it ended with, "Good boy, I tell you, just stay until we go on the Christmas trip. I don't care where your consciousness goes. Just make it to the Christmas trip."

By this time in the conversation, we had walked into Guru's room. Another boy, Unmilan, was busy setting up some weight-lifting apparatus while our conversation continued. Seeing something was wrong, he took it upon himself to invite me to lunch after Guru dismissed the both of us. What a good and supportive friend he was then and remains even now. We talked and he empathized with me, and encouraged and inspired me.

I returned to my room and meditated there. I felt Guru so powerfully, and the pain ebbed. I decided then and there not to leave.

At the appointed hour, I met Guru in the lobby for a drive to a music store. When I saw him, I said, "You win Guru. I lose. You don't have to come into my boat. Let me stay in yours." Immediately Guru started to sing one of his Bengali songs, *"Hari jadi ma tor kache, seito amar joy.* Mother, if I lose to You this is my only victory. Come."

That evening after the concert, I was massaging Guru in the function in front of all the students, many of whom were newly accepted. After Guru left, I was surrounded by these newer students with questions. They were obviously deluded by the appearance. Here I was driving Guru around, escorting him everywhere, massaging him. Little did they know that only that morning I had given Guru my letter.

So, appearances can be deluding. We don't know what is happening. We assume outer closeness must mean inner closeness, and this is not at all true. In fact, in 2006, I heard Guru mention that the student who was making the fastest progress was now living in Russia, and had yet to actually see Guru personally! Clearly, the reality of the inner relationship counts for everything and not the appearance created by the outer relationship.

❖ "Just who am I working on?"

Occasionally I had the opportunity to be with Guru alone in his home. On these rare occasions, I tried especially hard not to "pull" on him, so that he could relax, rest, or do whatever he wanted to.

On this particular occasion, Guru was on the massage table face down. He made a pillow of his arms and was in a light sleep. Now, a spiritual Master's sleep is different than typical sleep in the way you or I might do. What seems to happen—and this is totally my interpretation—is that the body is allowed to sleep while the Master travels off into some other plane of consciousness.

This was certainly true for Guru. The evidence of this is that when Guru would eventually wake from a rest, he was aware of what that took place around him while he was sleeping.

So here I am sitting at Guru's feet, massaging him lightly because he seemed to be resting. I could see from Guru's slightly opened eyes that he was clearly in some meditative world. Something compelled me to break my intention to not bother Guru with questions. "Guru, may I ask you a question?"

With a voice that wasn't quite his, he acknowledged "Hmm." This was a yes.

"Guru," I said, "sometimes you invite me to massage you, and I know I am not in the best consciousness, and I'm certain that you will feel much worse when I am done. Does this ever bother you?"

With a voice that can only be described as coming from another world altogether came his reply, "Nothing touches me, nothing touches me."

I had the thought, "God, just who am I working on?"

❖ Guru's pain and Ongkar's pain

Every April, Guru's students would gather in New York to be with him to celebrate the anniversary of Guru's arrival in New York from India–April 13. It was there that I first met my good friend Ongkar in 1980, under unfortunate circumstances. He had severe sciatica and there was some question as to whether he should come to New York from London for these April festivities. Guru told him to come. Later when I was sitting with Guru, he told me, "When Ongkar comes, you please take care of him. I will work through you."

I remember well Ongkar's arrival. We were all at Martin Van Buren High School. We used the school's gymnasium as a Friday evening meeting place. I was working on Guru's leg when Ongkar arrived, and he was writhing in pain. He was being supported under both arms, his leg was folded up under him and his face was both grimacing in pain and showing exhaustion. I immediately rushed over to escort him into the men's locker room where there was a couch.

I reported his condition to Guru, who then walked into the locker room where he greeted Ongkar and proceeded to meditate on him.

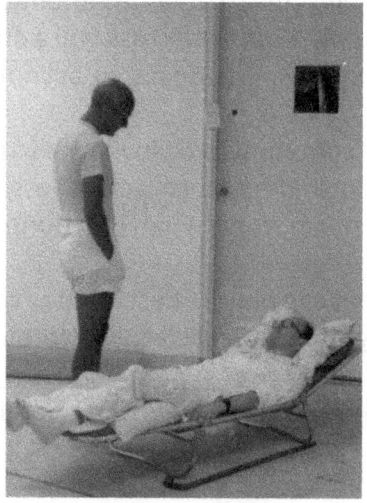

Meditating on Ongkar's painful leg.

As he meditated, it was obvious that Guru was concentrating on his pain. His meditative gaze repeatedly moved up and down Ongkar's leg. After a few minutes, Guru affirmed to Ongkar, "You will be all right in a few days."

Guru returned to his chair and I was called again to Guru's feet.

"You saw me walk over to Ongkar?" Guru asked.

"Yes, Guru."

"You saw me meditate and enter into his pain?"

"Yes, Guru."

"I wish to tell you that my pain is one thousand times worse than his, only I have a little more capacity to deal with it."

At the Feet of my Master

❖ Making faces

I treated Ongkar quite regularly at that time, and as a result, became quite close with his wife, Vinodini, and two daughters, Shankara and Dipika, who were nine and six years old respectively at the time. Both Shankara and Dipika are wonderful singers, and their very first performance was during this visit. As fate would have it, I was massaging Guru during their premiere performance. Oh God, I am very bad. As they were singing, I kept turning around to make faces at them. To their credit, they struggled but maintained their composure.

Subsequent to this, I was always greeted very warmly by the two of them, and this was inevitably followed by a friendly punch in my stomach. They have since grown out of that habit, but I know they lived in fear of the possibility that I would be at Guru's feet when they performed.

Over the years, from time to time, Sri Chinmoy would invite these two girls to take dictation of poems and prayers, or to sing songs with their larger singing group. And, if I happened to have been there massaging Guru, a huge grin would come over my face while they had to concentrate extra hard on Guru!

❖ Ongkar's passing

It is impossible to speak about Ongkar without mentioning that on February 28, 2006, my dear and good brother-friend passed. I was blessed to play an intimate part in his final months.

Every Christmas season, Guru and literally hundreds of his students would travel to a different part of the world for a combination "vacation, spiritual retreat, cultural exchange". These annual events came to be known as our "Christmas Trips", and grew to 3 months in length! I've had the great experience of visiting some 40 to 50 countries on these trips.

The Christmas trip in 2005, Ongkar's last, brought us to Malaysia. When he first arrived, there was very little sign of his health crisis. As his health degenerated, myself along with 3 or 4 other boys, and of course Ongkar's wife, Vinodini, and his daughters all shared caretaking roles.

While Ongkar and I did not have the opportunity to spend a lot of time together because we were separated by an ocean, inwardly I always felt closer than the closest to him. I knew I always had a friend in him, and he felt the same for me. It was only a few years ago that Ongkar received his first "special blessing" from Guru…yes, a scolding. I was honored that he called me for consolation. I told him, "Congratulations! Your Guru really loves you!"

His battle with a brain tumor slowly took away his motor skills, speaking skills and strength. He would pass in and out of lucidity. I spent many private hours with him, during which time we would chat and laugh.

I was the captain of the "shower team". The boys would escort Ongkar into the washroom for his morning shower, and I would then jump in with swimming trunks, lather Ongkar up, and then towel him down. Once I said to him, "Ongkar, we've been dear friends many years." He nodded an acknowledgement. "And I bet in your wildest imagination you never thought we'd be doing this together!" We both laughed.

I think that my most memorable moment of that experience has to be running with Ongkar. Our last stop on that unforgetable vacation took us to Langkawi, Malaysia. Twice a week the group had a morning "fun run" of 1 or 2 miles. I had the honor of running while pushing Ongkar in his wheel chair. Everyone called his name, and when we crossed the finish line, everyone was cheering "Ongkar, Ongkar, Ongkar…!" Tears came to his eyes. Guru greeted him with the broadest smile. I miss my brother…my brother, Ongkar.

❖ What's in Guru's back pocket?

Once, when Guru was in his running years, he traveled to San Francisco to participate in the marathon that the Centre was sponsoring. Nirvik and I rode in a car, trailing Guru a little bit, just in case he got cramps in his calves, which was apt to happen.

At the Feet of my Master

In fact, he would refer to these regularly-timed cramps as his "friends", saying, "Always at mile fourteen, my friends come and greet me."

During a short section of the running route, however, the car could not follow, so I got out of the car and ran with or slightly behind Guru, while the car proceeded forward to meet Guru on the route a little later on. As fate would have it, Guru's "friends" came and greeted him quite nicely during this time.

Guru's left calf tightened up, stopping Guru from running. I ran up to Guru and immediately started working on his calf muscle. "Good boy, good boy," Guru said through a pained expression. "I tell you, if you get rid of these cramps, I will give you your realization much sooner!"

Unfortunately, I didn't. But it struck me that Guru seemed to have my realization in his back pocket and he could give it to me whenever he wanted to!

Running with Guru during the San Francisco Centre Marathon just in case his "friends" visited him.

At the Feet of my Master

❖ Running into a cop during the NYC Marathon

Although this doesn't have anything to do with dialoguing with Guru directly, this is one of those incidents that only seemed to happen when Guru was around. One year, Guru began the New York City Marathon three hours early. Sadly, his marathon time had slowed considerably due to ever-increasing leg pain, so he decided to start early so that he might finish with the pack. Along with a few other boys, I was invited to escort Guru by running behind him. This way, in case any police questioned why he was on the course so early, I could use my "Doctor" credentials to explain his presence and why the boys were accompanying him.

As it turned out, my presence was not needed because the Achilles Track Club had special permission to start early, so there were many runners on the course at that time. Everything was going along fine. Guru was running with a team of three or four boys following. It was in fact these boys who drew the attention of one policeman. He was parked in his car along with his partner. As Guru and his entourage passed we heard, "Hey, what are you guys doing on the course?"

"Uh oh," I thought to myself, and turned to the police car ready to explain our presence. I looked at the policeman and recognizing his face asked, "Don't I know you?"

"Balter?" he replied.

I couldn't believe it. The one and only cop who questioned us on the course was my cousin!

6

Sagas from the Concert World

One of the duties that Sri Chinmoy asked me (and many others) to perform was to organize concerts for him. In 1984, to express his gratitude to the West for allowing him to be of service for 20 years, Guru decided to offer a series of twenty musical concerts. At these concerts, Guru performed on various musical instruments with interludes of silent meditation. Guru's concerts became a regular and important part of his own personal service to humanity.

Sri Chinmoy once told me that in these concerts he brought down a consciousness which was absolutely new to the earth plane, and he planted a seed of joy in each seeker who attended. Later—it may be ten minutes, a few weeks, months or even a few years—that seeker would feel a sense of joy emanating from his heart. He may not associate it with the concert at all, nor is that important.

Sagas from the Concert World

As you read through the first few stories here, you may wonder what they have to do with concert giving. They are another example of seemingly non-congruent moments being connected to provide some ultimate lesson.

❖ The concert challenge (part 1)

Towards the end of the 1990-91 Christmas trip in Bali, Guru called three students—Nayak, Ketan and myself—to his side while he himself was exercising. This was our second trip to Bali, staying at the Sanur Beach Hotel. Guru made a very specific request of us and invited us to take up the challenge. Guru invited each of us to put on a concert, but there was a "BUT" attached to his request.

When assigning a concert, typically Guru would set a goal based on his vision of how many people were inwardly "ready" to come, along with the principles of transcendence. For example, if one year's concert brought 1,000 seekers, then for the next year's concert Guru might set a goal of 2,000, and so on, and so on.

Up until this point, however, America as a whole had never succeeded in fulfilling Guru's vision. If the goal was 4,000 people, perhaps 2,000 would come. If the goal was 2,000, then 1,200 might come. This phenomenon was usually accompanied with "we tried our best but..."

This time would be different. Guru told us that the goal for each concert was to be 7,000 and that we had to wholeheartedly embrace his vision. If we did so, then we would easily achieve the goal. Guru placed before us a challenge—to embrace his vision or not do a concert. If we felt that we were not going to succeed, then he would prefer us to not do the concert and perhaps try another time. But Guru was emphatic that the task could be easily achieved if we inwardly identified with him.

He added that he would not be displeased with us at all if we chose to not take up the challenge, or alternatively, if we should accept the challenge but later cancel the event because we were

Sagas from the Concert World

not going to achieve the goal. Finally, he told us that we could hold these concerts anywhere we wanted, that is, we weren't bound to our home cities.

All three of us took up the challenge. Nayak's concert was to be in Seattle, Ketan chose Atlanta, and I decided to stay put in Chicago. Now, let me qualify that calling a concert "Nayak's" or "Ketan's" is an inappropriate euphemism. These were all "American" concerts that required the support of everyone.

❖ I would go there myself

Upon returning from the Christmas trip in 1991, Guru and I were greeted with the sad news that two boys, Amiya and Sartaknama, had both left the path. I include myself with Guru because I knew both of these fellows extremely well. Besides being fellow chiropractors, it happens that they were also both my students at the National College of Chiropractic, where I taught.

I was feeling sad that two friends had left. At the time, both these boys served the Marathon Team by being jointly in charge of medical service at the races. I am embarrassed to admit that one of my first thoughts upon hearing of their departure was, "Oh God, I hope Guru is not going to ask me to be in charge of medical at the races." I had actually stopped practicing chiropractic and had gotten pretty "touched out" from my practice, so this was not a job that I relished.

At the tennis court, Guru called me to massage him. "So, two chiropractors have left."

"Yes," I affirmed.

Then, most lovingly and affectionately, he looked down at me and said, "If you should ever leave me, even if you were to go halfway around the world, I would go there myself to retrieve you."

Oh God, Guru, as I replay this moment in my mind, I realize that you are just trying to conquer us all with your love power. Please Guru, the sooner the better.

❖ The concert challenge (part 2)

The Seattle concert was the first to be scheduled—and the first to be canceled. I had heard that, after informing Guru of the cancelation, Nayak was walking the streets of Seattle in tears, such was his disappointment. Upon officially canceling the concert, Guru offered Nayak the opportunity to take two more weeks if they felt they might succeed. The folks working there accepted Guru's offer. Sadly though, success was not to be theirs. Only a few thousand attended.

The next scheduled concert and the next to be canceled was the Chicago concert. I did not react the way Nayak did, and as such felt that perhaps I was inadequate. Anyway, on being informed that we were canceling our event, Guru sent the message that we would not get a second chance as Seattle had. So be it, I thought, the task is done.

Perhaps two days later, I got a call from Nishtha. She was at Guru's home and was calling with a message from Guru. "Guru wants to know how quickly you can pack your bags," she said. I thought to myself, "Okay, Guru's finally had it with me. I have failed for the last time and it's time for a change in leadership." After a moment's thought, I replied, "Well, I guess I could leave tomorrow." There was a pause during which time Nishtha conveyed my response to Guru.

Finally, Nishtha told me Guru's reply. "That's fine. Please come to New York to be in charge of medical for the race." The moment I dreaded had come true, but I was greatly relieved nevertheless.

❖ Humility is the key

I arrived in New York the next day and went directly to the race. Shortly thereafter, Guru arrived and was driven around the course. At seeing me, he kindly waved. Eventually, he made his way to his little gazebo at the course and I was called in. The conversation eventually turned to the recently canceled Chicago concert. I confessed to feeling badly that I didn't react to the cancelation of the concert as Nayak did, and I asked Guru if something was wrong with me. Guru said, "Has discouragement ever helped anybody, anytime, anywhere?"

A short time later, a small dog passed in front of Guru's house. Guru said, "Now I am going to tell you the key to succeed. Did you see that dog just walk across?"

"Yes, Guru."

"You have to have the humility of the grass. A small dog can walk or the president can walk on it. In either case, with utmost humility, the grass simply offers itself. This is the key.

When we give a concert, it should not be that we are doing something so special that people have to come. No. It should be that we are grateful for the opportunity to be of service to them, to their aspiration. Now, September 13th will be your date. You must succeed, you must succeed, you must succeed."

I sensed in Guru's request both a plea and a command. America needed a successful concert, and at the same time, the Supreme in Guru commanded it.

Fortunately, by virtue of the hard work of students all across America, success did come. Six thousand, eight hundred people came to the UIC Pavilion in Chicago. Guru said there were at least 200 inner beings in attendance, so he considered the event a success.

❖ The 1992 concert

The 1991 concert was a tremendous amount of work, and it challenged me on many, many levels. It entailed enlisting and managing a hundred people, raising funds, making phone calls and many "all-nighters." Up to that point, it had been the pattern that a new concert director was selected for each year's major concert, so I was looking forward to having a more relaxed 1992!

Shortly after returning from the Christmas trip of that year, Guru announced at a meeting that, from that point, only those who had already put on a successful concert would be asked to direct concerts. Remember that the previous year's American concert was the first one deemed successful by Guru. This was

Sagas from the Concert World

confirmed by Guru himself when he added, "So in America, if Pradhan wants to do a concert, he can do, otherwise there will be no concert this year in America."

Oh God, what could I do? I must confess that part of me was reluctant to take on the task, but on the other hand, there had to be a concert in America. I quickly wrote Guru a note saying that if he wanted a concert, of course I would do it, but there was a large "But!" attached to the note. I wanted Guru to know that I had other plans. They were good plans, but did not include a concert. At that time, I was giving a lot of classes in America, and they were meeting with good success in inspiring people, so I informed Guru of my plan to visit every Centre across the U.S. to give as many talks as I could.

Upon receiving my note, Guru immediately called me in front of him. All he talked about was the concert. "Where will you do it? I want to do someplace new, someplace I have not been." We talked about different possibilities and Guru liked Texas as the location, so Texas it was.

Just to be sure that Guru had read my note and to give Guru the opportunity to reassign me, I mentioned my "But!" to Guru. "Guru, I just want to make it clear that I had hoped to visit every Centre and give classes on meditation." The only responses I had considered were either, "No, do the concert" or "Yes, that is a better thing to do...someone else can do the concert." Guru, of course, came up with a different response: "Can you not do both?"

In October of 1992, some 7,800 people came to see Guru at the University of Houston. The success of this concert was due to a wonderful collaboration of American and international students, which pleased Guru very much.

❖ The 1993 concert

By way of background, in 1893, the Parliament of the World's Religions met in Chicago as part of the World Exposition being held there. Of course, this was when the great Swami

Sagas from the Concert World

Vivekananda first became known to America. (Guru has written and spoken much on Swami Vivekananda. My sense is that they are like inner "brothers".)

In 1993, one hundred years later, a second Parliament of the World's Religions was being convened in Chicago. Guru was invited to open that event with seven minutes of meditation. I think that Guru himself considered this to be one of his most auspicious manifestations. And of course, there was talk of Vivekananda all that year.

Early in 1993, there was no talk of a concert, only the Parliament. I confess I was relieved by this. I was in Ottawa for a work-related event when I received a call from Ashrita with a message from Guru. "Vivekananda's soul came to me. He said that he lived 39 years on earth, so he has requested me to offer 39 concerts. The last concert has to be in Chicago and should be for 13,000 people."

"Oh...okay," came my not-so-enthusiastic reply.

A few minutes later the phone rang again. It was Ashrita with an addendum. He told me, "Guru said that Vivekananda actually wanted 39,000 people, but your soul immediately came to Guru and said that you would die a thousand deaths."

My soul was correct.

I mentioned that April brings Guru's students to New York. Well, we actually gather twice a year. In August of every year, Guru's students gather in New York in celebration of his August 27th birthday. This is a 2-week event which includes meditations, runs, performances, singing and more. It is two weeks of inspiration. But 1993 was a very unique experience. Guru's actual birthday event ended early and most of us packed up and left New York for Chicago on August 28th. Guru opened the 100th Anniversary of the Parliament of the World's Religions with a seven-minute meditation. This was an absolutely wonderful event and experience.

At that opening event, I swear Guru brought God down in front of thousands of people in absolute silence. The rest of the people who shared the opening dais with Guru just talked and talked and talked.

I was so proud of Guru, and equally proud to be escorting him around the crowd. I was in the elevator when a woman noticed me and recognized me as the individual escorting Guru. She said, "I wish he had meditated more and everybody else had talked less!"

"Me too!" I thought to myself as I smiled in acknowledgement.

Guru came twice to Chicago that year. Just two weeks after the Parliament, Guru returned to Chicago to offer the concert that Vivekananda requested. In his honor, we called it the Oneness-World Vivekananda Peace Concert. That concert was a difficult concert. Sadly, only 4,500 people attended.

❖ The 27,000 concert (part 1)

I believe Guru saw that the task of directing the concerts was taking a toll on me. Allow me to confess that as of this writing, some 15 years later, it is incorrect to blame the task for the struggle. It is honest to say my reluctance to perform the task was responsible for my struggle. This was made clear during the span between 1996 and 2001, a period I have dubbed "The 27,000 concert years."

In the years immediately following the 1993 Vivekananda Concert, Guru assigned two other directors to head up concerts. In 1994, my spiritual sister, Suprabha, directed a concert in Washington D.C. where close to 9,000 attended; and in 1995, two other students, Pragati and Bahula, directed the Philadelphia Peace Concert where some 9,500 people attended. For my part, I had almost nothing to do with these concerts except to aid in some fundraising.

Let me share with you that for a concert director, the minutes just preceding the concert itself is an experience of intense anticipation and stress. You've invested months of time, spent lots of money and it all comes down to this short period when you see if the actual concert is a success in terms of achieving your goals.

Sagas from the Concert World

In the 1993 concert, when I was backstage with Guru, he watched me pacing and pacing as people entered the concert hall. "Good boy, just surrender," was his soothing advice. "It is all done. There is nothing more for you to do!" The absurdity of this stress is easy to see after it is all said and done, but those minutes before the concert begins are "special", let me assure you.

This was, I believe, true for Pragati in Philadelphia. I can recall standing in the backstage area of the Philadelphia concert. (It was very nice to serve as an observer.) Every 10 minutes or so, as the concert opening drew near, Pragati would check on how many people had arrived at that point. This is what one does—pace, then check attendance, pace some more, then check attendance!

The concert hall was extremely slow to fill because the Philadelphia 76er's (Philly's basketball team) had a game the same night and shared the parking lot with the concert hall. As a result, driving congestion was intense and people were slow to get into the concert hall. I could read the angst on Pragati's face as she would say, "There seems to be only 3,000," or "4,000". Indeed, at the scheduled time of 8 p.m. only 4,500 people were in the hall. It seemed to me that Pragati's face was filled with disappointment. I may have been projecting—I have never asked her—but watching and empathizing was painful. Inwardly, silently, I swore that I would never do another concert.

Fortunately, for my sister Pragati, another 5,000 people entered the hall in the next half hour! But my promise had already been made. Guru has a favorite aphorism, "Man proposes, God disposes." A few months later, my promise would soon be challenged.

While a concert of 9,500 was wonderfully successful and represented America's largest concert to date, America still lagged behind the rest of the world with regards to concert attendance. For example, 13,000 people had attended concerts in Europe and Canada. Well, in August of 1996, during Guru's Birthday week, I had the opportunity to spend a lot of time with Guru, both publicly in my role as masseur and privately escorting Guru here or there. As it turns out, Guru had an appointment to see a Russian doctor in Manhattan who would work on Guru's knee. Pulak drove while I sat in the back seat. I watched the Russian doctor work as he applied extremely and painfully deep pressure on points around Guru's knee. By observing, I could attempt to reproduce the treatment should it have provided relief.

After the appointment, Pulak, Guru and I returned to Pulak's parked car to discover that the battery was dead. We were parked at a Manhattan street meter. This predated mass cell phone distribution, so Pulak went off to call for some roadside help and I moved from my backseat position to the driver's seat so that the car appeared to be clearly attended.

When you spend this amount of time with Guru, you find yourself pretty "warmed up". Any reluctance which might usually be there is melted away, so it seems. Guru began a conversation.

"Good boy, next year, I really want you to concentrate on manifestation."

My seemingly soulful readiness came to the fore. "Yes Guru," I said with folded hands.

"Next year, I really want America to come to the fore. Why should America lag behind the rest of the world? America is so strong, so dynamic..."

I was into it. "Yes Guru," came my enthusiastic, hands-folded reply.

"So good boy, next year I want you to do a concert for 27,000."

In a moment, all the soulfulness flew out the door. With a quick head shift, I turned to Guru and said, "Are you serious?" I said this so spontaneously, I don't think I even realized it!

Guru didn't miss a beat, and compassionately chose to ignore my sudden shift in temperament. "Of course I am serious, but where will you do?"

Guru had me where he wanted me for the moment. "Denver?" came my spontaneous reply, which had some tone of a question to it.

"Very good, very good. Someplace new, very good."
"But Guru, may I take some time to investigate sites, because I don't know if Denver has a venue that can hold this amount."
"Definitely."

I will never forget that moment. It was a moment of enthusiasm, excitement and thrill, nicely blended with a little hiccup of "Oh my God!" Yes, a gurgle of fear-filled reluctance.

It took me a few days to digest the magnitude of the task. Normally in a concert cycle, you communicate with the rest of the student community via either a Centre leader or some other individual who has shown previous enthusiasm for the task. This time, however, I felt the task to be so big that I asked Guru if I could visit other Centres to garner the necessary support. He approved and off I went. I have to say that experiencing the Centres and community of people who make them up was a wonderful experience. We have a beautiful family. I felt the leap from 9,500 to 27,000 would require a whole new approach to concert giving. It was not obvious to me how to do it. I was looking for inspiration. I was looking for partnership. I was, frankly, looking for help.

After some time and research, we had decided that Minneapolis would be the actual location. As time went on, however, I confess that my gurgle of fear had become a steady stream. The task seemed overwhelming, and as the end-of-year Christmas trip approached, I began not sleeping well. I would occasionally wake up with a list of things to do. Inside me, a growing turmoil was brewing. Part of me did not want to do this concert. Part of me was very afraid of the task—the size of task, the responsibility—whatever—but the reluctance grew. During the Christmas trip in Japan, I would hear comments from others, like, "How come we're not hearing about the 27,000 concert?"

"Oh we're working on it," I would say, but in fact, I didn't want to talk about it.

When I returned to Chicago, things only got worse. I experienced a horrible blend of fear and reluctance. The stream had become a river. Sleepless nights came more often, coming to a peak in April. One night during the ensuing April Celebrations, I woke up with an amazing tension and because other people were sleeping in the same room, I couldn't put on any lights. I lay in my bed, and the situation got worse and worse. I felt I was going to break mentally.

It was about 12:30 a.m. I had to do something, so I quietly got dressed, slipped out, got into my car and drove in front of Guru's house. I stopped there and just prayed and prayed. (Let me note…this was not a good thing to do. I was invading Guru's physical space without permission, but I was out of control.) While I was there, Guru must have sensed something, because amazingly he peered out his window and saw the car. When I saw him do that, I slowly drove away, ending up at a local diner. I ordered a rice pudding and hot chocolate and sat reading a newspaper. The combination of Guru's awareness and comfort food settled me down. I went home and back to bed, knowing that the next morning I had to talk to Ashrita to tell him what was going on.

About 8 a.m. I called Ashrita and told him what I was experiencing, that I felt I was on the verge of a nervous breakdown. He did his duty, reporting it to Guru, and returned with a message quite quickly. Guru said, "This thing that you did is not good, not good. There are wrong forces all around you. No student of mine is worth losing for any manifestation. I am canceling the concert." I greeted this message with both a sense of relief and remorse. Quickly, the tension of it all disappeared as Guru put a very powerful force on me. But I had failed, failed Guru, failed America–failed.

I couldn't even get the concert started, really. And just in case I wasn't wounded enough, that night at an evening function, the Czech students all got up on the stage. They announced how proud they were that their American student brothers and sisters were taking up the challenge of a 27,000 concert. Then they sang Guru's "America" song, beautifully and powerfully. I walked out mid-song. They did not know–that very morning Guru had canceled the concert.

Sagas from the Concert World

❖ The 27,000 concert (part 2)

The Minneapolis Centre was, as one would expect, very inspired about having such a landmark event in its backyard, and in the coming years assumed responsibility for the concert. Unfortunately, for various reasons, this concert struggled to get off the drawing board. Finally, in 2001, Guru asked me if I was ready to do a concert again. I responded that I would like to have another go at the 27,000 in Minneapolis, and he agreed. I knew it would mean facing my demons again. I thought I was ready to give it a shot.

Facing my demons is an accurate description. Nandita, who was assigned to the concert as well, and I set up shop in Minneapolis. Fundraising began, posters were designed and off we went. Only one thing was missing: co-workers to help with the concert were not forthcoming.

After two months of working, still there were only the two of us. In hindsight, I realized that I was, in fact, projecting my issues onto my brother and sister students, and therefore I did not invite them to come to Minneapolis with the right sense of urgency. My fears began to resurface. There was more. The only hall we could afford was the brand new Excel Arena in St. Paul which only held 18,000. This meant that the concert was beginning to shrink in scope, and with that, self-doubt and disappointment were being added to my inner mix.

❖ The squirrel and the crow

While in Minneapolis, I was hosted by one of the Minneapolis students, Meghabhuti. For those of you who may not know him, Meghabhuti is one of the most optimistic people I know. He sees beauty in everyone and everything.

One night I was awakened by Meghabhuti. He was kneeling at my bedside. "Pradhan, Pradhan, you're having a nightmare," he told me. Indeed, I remembered screaming in my dream, "No! No! No!" This woke him.

"Get up and meditate," he said, "and then we're going for a walk." At the time, Meghabhuti lived in a beautiful little neighborhood of Minneapolis. We were walking through some nearby parks when Meghabhuti spotted a white squirrel. "Oh, that's a great omen," he told me, and then went on to narrate the story of Rama and Sita. "Not only did the monkeys aid in Rama's mission, but the squirrels helped also," Meghabhuti explained, "so squirrels are good omens. And, a white squirrel is especially good! Now crows, on the other hand, especially cawing crows—those are bad omens."

Now, while I appreciate omens and that sort of thing, I don't give them much importance. I told Meghabhuti that on the way to the concert office in the morning, there are always cawing crows! He assured me that the white squirrel meant that today would be different. Meghabhuti succeeded in cheering me up. We returned to his home and he then left for work. A few minutes later, I left as well for the concert office, and what did I witness on the road just next to my car? A squirrel—a dead squirrel in fact, being ravaged by two screaming crows. I had to laugh. "There go my omens," I thought to myself!

❖ A spiritual transfusion

Shortly thereafter, I realized preparations for the concert were barely moving. The pieces were all in place, but the intensity and workers were missing. Personally I was not doing well either. My demons had become my life partners. It felt as though there was fear running through my veins. I was starting to spiral downward and wrote Guru a note as such. Guru responded quickly. "I have read your letter. Come to New York for a few days." I promptly did.

If there is such a thing as a spiritual blood transfusion, Guru performed it. Within two days, my fear-filled arteries were carrying spiritual oxygen again and I felt much better. I returned to Minneapolis. Nandita quickly embarked on the task of getting other disciples to work on the concert. They came and took to the task. We had a beautiful concert of 8,500 in St. Paul. It was not 27,000, but it came with a valuable lesson.

In hindsight, I am amazed at the power that my fear and reluctance had over me. It paralyzed me in more ways than one. We tend to see the world through the lenses of our own life experiences. My reluctance caused me to assume others were also reluctant, so I simply didn't ask for the help I needed. Guru constantly asked us to be heroes in the battlefield of life. While it appears that it was the concert itself that was the cause of my fear, this was not true at all. It only served to bring my own inner reluctance and fear to the fore. My role, indeed all of our roles as students, is to act... to act with devotion, without "attachment" to the outcome. It was my own personal attachment to the success of the concert that caused me to have this fear. Indeed, it is this inner battlefield where the most difficult battles are fought. I believe I have learned that lesson—yes, I hope so.

7

The Great Pizza Wars

Dedicated to my dearest friend Sunil

The precise manner in which the Great Pizza Wars began, I cannot exactly say. I can only say that these wars were "bloody" and lasted for years, and that Guru found himself in the middle of them. The wars began shortly after I became a student in 1971. I had one year of school left at Northwestern University. It was then, for the first time, I had the experience of Chicago deep dish pan pizza (commonly known as "pan pizza"). Now I must confess that up until this point, like my New York brethren, I was completely unliberated with regards to pizza. You see, New Yorkers are extremely attached to their pizza, and anything that is a departure from New York pizza simply "ain't pizza". Somehow, "Sicilian style" has successfully made its way into the New York pizza culture, but this is an aberration of sorts.

The Great Pizza Wars

The fact is that Chicago has the highest consumption of pizza per capita in the world[1]. In Chicago, there are three styles of pizza: thin crust, deep dish or "pan" pizza, and stuffed pizza. New York pizza would be considered a variety of thin crust pizza. Deep dish is the signature pizza of Chicago. New York's Sicilian pizza might be compared to deep dish, but it is a pathetic imitation. Stuffed pizza stands on its own. Stuffed pizza is about 1.5-2 inches thick. There is a bottom crust, then filling including cheese, and finally a top crust over which the sauce and fresh tomatoes and herbs are placed.

My favorite is deep dish, although I confess that as I've gotten older, I've rediscovered the lightness of thin crust. I also went through my stuffed pizza phase. Let me also say that I love New York pizza. But I unequivocally stand by my assertion that if forced to choose one, Chicago deep dish pan pizza is far, far superior to New York pizza—an assertion which I did not hesitate to share with my brother and sister students in New York.

And so the wars began.

❖ **"What, no pizza?"**

Upon returning to New York after completion of my schooling in Chicago, somehow the word went around my fellow students that I preferred Chicago pizza to New York pizza. Apparently this was a source of consternation to many New Yorkers. My suspicion is that it actually struck at the heart of their faith. And somehow this whole debate made it to Guru. It was 1982. I was in New York for my birthday.

After meditation, Guru would typically offer a light food. The food offered after meditation is called "prasad." And, it is also traditional for special occasions to provide such prasad. I ar-

---

1 My Italian friend, Priyadarshan, read this and immediately broke into a fever. "Apparently your world does not include Italy."

The Great Pizza Wars

ranged to bring Dunkin' Donuts for my birthday prasad. Out of the blue Guru said, "What, you could not bring pizza?" So be it.

That night I had thirteen stuffed pizzas flown in from Chicago. The function went extra late in anticipation of the event. The pizza arrived, was reheated at Annam Brahma Restaurant and served to mixed reviews. "It's good, but it's not pizza!" came the cries. Some liked it, some didn't. Some secretly came to tell me they liked it much better, but they were afraid, very afraid (I joke!).

Guru was publicly noncommittal, but privately he told me he liked it better. I suspect privately he told the New Yorkers he liked theirs better.

Ever since then, I have been forever linked with pizza; and in fact, pizza has played a large and fun role in many interesting experiences.

❖ The Venezuela pizza experience

Of all the students to rally to the cause of New York pizza, my spiritual brother Sunil was the most outspoken. This debate became a source of great joy for the both of us. During the Christmas trip in Venezuela we stayed at one particular hotel which required you to go to the operator to make a long distance call. I wanted to call home and Sunil escorted me over to the long distance operator.

"I'd like to call the United States please," I said.

"What city in the United States?" she asked with a fairly thick accent.

Jokingly, I said, "Oh, the city with the best pizza in the world."

She thought for a minute and then said, "Oh, you must mean Chicago!"

Sunil shook his head in disbelief. It was a great victory.

The Great Pizza Wars

❖ The Mormon pizza experience

During the 1984-85 Christmas trip, our first stop was in Torremolinos, Spain. During these earlier Christmas trips, we actually cooked for ourselves instead of having the hotels provide food. Here we were using the kitchens of the Mormon Church.

All young men of the Mormon Church are required to offer two years of service as "Elders". As Elders, they go to different places around the globe and proselytize. Their task is to convert the non-believers. Because we were using their church, we each knew about the other. We were the guys who dressed in white. The Elders dressed in black. All the Elders I had met were visiting from the United States.

That year, the Chicago Bears were coming into their own as a football team. In fact, the following year they won the Super Bowl. Because of their success, I was particularly interested in the games that Christmas.

One afternoon, I was passing by a local pizza place and a group of Elders were sitting at an open window. I yelled up, "Hey, any of you guys know the football scores?" Which they in fact did, so they replied with what they knew. About ten minutes later, I stopped by this same pizza place for lunch. I sat at a table by myself, but the remaining tables were all filled with Elders. I guess it was lunch break.

At any rate, the fellows whom I had asked about the football scores were sitting right in front of me and they very kindly invited me to join them for lunch and conversation, which I gladly did.

Well, one of the fellows at the table, Elder John, was obviously the elder Elder, and he started to engage me in conversation on our beliefs. It was very clear that it was his intention to convert me. He was going to show the rest of the younger Elders how it could be done. I was to be their first "catch" from our group.

"So tell me," Elder John asked, "do you believe in the resurrection?" With this, the entire restaurant became somewhat silent. Here were twenty-five elders in black and one Sri Chinmoy student in white. The intent was immediately clear from the question. He wasn't curious— he was at work.

Well, as those of you who know me will attest, I can talk with the best of them, so off I went into a lecture on the value of the resurrection, death, reincarnation, etc. I am also quite good at maintaining a diplomatic and accepting attitude, honoring the beliefs of others while I espouse my own. I held my own, but I was definitely feeling uncomfortable. I just wanted to enjoy a pizza and some friendship.

After I answered the Elder's first question, the next question came. "But you do accept Jesus as the only true Son of God, don't you?" Off I went again explaining the difference between my beliefs and the beliefs of most Christians, supporting my beliefs with quotes from various scriptures.

Since they ordered before me, in the middle of my answer their pizzas arrived, and without any hesitation they dug right into them as if they hadn't eaten in days. I kept on talking, still very much aware of Elder John's intent.

A few minutes later, my pizza arrived. I paused mid-sentence and said, "Will you gentlemen excuse me for just a minute?" Then I bowed my head and prayed as soulfully as I possibly could. The entire restaurant, having been an audience to this conversation, was forced to stop eating while I prayed. I have never prayed as soulfully in front of my food as I did that afternoon. I prayed for at least two minutes and had an intense vision of Guru's face over the table. Meanwhile, all of the Elders were waiting for me to finish. When I felt secure in Guru's heart, I finally raised my head, smiled, and started to eat.

Elder John looked at me. There was a pause. "So," he finally said with a new tone, "any of you guys play basketball?"

❖ **One piece of pizza, one new student**

My home has always served as the Centre, so when I attended chiropractic school, the Chicago Centre was in fact located in the western suburb of Villa Park, and not in Chicago proper. Across

The Great Pizza Wars

the street from where I lived was an absolutely wonderful Middle Eastern restaurant. One would not normally expect pizza to be served in such a restaurant, but they did serve it, and it was excellent by any standard. I ate there regularly and became very good friends with the owners.

One evening, as I was enjoying a pizza there, an Indian woman walked by my table and I overheard her express surprise to her friend at seeing pizza being served at a Middle Eastern restaurant. I also heard her say that it looked delicious. Having overheard this, and being a proponent of good pizza, I grabbed a small plate and brought a slice of my pizza over to her table.

Well, she was quite surprised and delighted and tried not to accept it, but I insisted, saying I would get joy in sharing it with her. She did eat it and she enjoyed it. Afterwards, she approached me and thanked me but, perhaps more importantly, she said that she had never met anyone who had ever done anything like that before. She introduced herself and inquired as to what I did. She was surprised that I had an Indian name and an Indian Guru. She expressed interest and later became a student. She spent many years on the path.

❖ **"Chicago pizza is by far the best!"**

In 1972, Sri Chinmoy invited the students to put on a circus. He asked us all to perform a simple act for the sake of creating joy. All sorts of hidden talents were revealed. New jugglers, clowns, fire-eaters and all kinds of other fun things were born! There was a time when practicing circus was a regular Friday night function in New York. Practices were often held at Martin Van Buren High School on Hillside Avenue. There were two back-to-back gymnasiums with Guru in one gym and everyone else practicing their circus act in the other. On one particular visit from Chicago, I was sitting and working on Guru along with another boy who was from New York. I was working on Guru's right leg, while my co-masseur was working on Guru's left. There were just the three of us.

The Great Pizza Wars

At a certain point, Guru began to go into another world. His meditation became quite intense. When this happens, quite naturally your massage becomes more devoted. There is the hope that some cosmic glitch might take place and with that you will suddenly become endowed with Guru's glorious consciousness.

Guru entered into a very high consciousness. Then he looked down upon the two of us with his meditative gaze. It was apparent that he was going to say something. Both of us looked up at Guru with anticipating eyes. What words was Guru going to utter from this other world?

With a sublime smile, Guru finally spoke, "Chicago pizza is by far the best!" and then his smile broadened. He knew he had taken us for a ride.

The message, however, was not lost on me. The next day I walked into a local student-owned eatery called "Smile of the Beyond." It was busy with customers. "Everyone," I blurted out. "I have an important announcement from Guru." The workers immediately attempted to hush me up. "No, it's too significant to pass up," I insisted.

"No, you can't do this. The public is here." I am sure that they anticipated that I was going to announce something akin to Ramakrishna's immortal utterance, "He who is Rama, he who is Krishna, in one body is Ramakrishna." But I insisted. When everyone was appropriately silent I announced, "Last night Guru said that Chicago pizza is by far the best."

The story does not end there. That night at the function, somehow the talk went to the pizza wars. I remember one of the New York boys standing up and saying, "Not only does Pradhan think it's better, but Guru, he said that you said it was better."

Guru said, "I did? When did I say?" I was about to remind Guru of the previous evening's experience, but then remembered the story that Guru once told about Arjuna seeing the world through Krishna's eyes. I thought to myself that I should agree with Guru.

The Great Pizza Wars

❖ **"I like it much better"**

In 1993, the Christmas trip again took us to Honolulu, Hawaii. I remember sampling pizza from a place called New York Pizza and it was a fairly good representation. It wasn't bad at all. Also in Honolulu was a place called "Pizzeria Uno-Chicago Pan Pizza." The original pan pizza restaurant in Chicago is in fact Pizzeria Uno. This has been franchised into a chain, but I must tell you that the franchise pizza bears very little resemblance to the original. I actually don't like it.

As fate would have it, one afternoon Guru asked for pizza for himself. Apparently two folks went out and got pizza from both New York Pizza and Pizzeria Uno to bring to Guru. After eating, Guru came out holding the box from Pizzeria Uno. "Pradhan, is this really Chicago pizza?"

"Well, yes Guru, but it's not the best."

"I like it much better!"

I was excited. "Guru, are you saying you like it better?"

"Yes, I like it much better!"

"It's over?" I asked.

"It's over," Guru confirmed.

Thank God, I thought. That was 1993. As of this writing, it is 2010. I know now—it will never be over.

8

Guru-isms

Guru just being Guru. I call these Guru-isms. They are moments of intense affection, compassion and wisdom. They are just moments, but carry a lifetime of meaning.

❖ **Guru's sweater gift**
Guru's best marathon was in Toledo, Ohio. He ran a 3:54 marathon. Because Chicago was somewhat nearby, the Chicago students planned a twenty-six course meal, which we cooked on site, to celebrate this event. After Guru's marathon, perhaps 100 of us were seated in front of Guru in a large meeting room. Someone presented Guru with a sweater that I felt was quite beautiful. Allow me to confess that I had the thought, "Gee, I wouldn't mind having a sweater like that." (Note: I place this under the "confession mode" because it is not proper to covet something that has been given to your Guru!)

As Guru was leaving for home from the hotel where he had a room, I was holding the front door open for him. He was carrying that sweater and that same thought came to me again. As he passed, Guru smiled at me and I at him and then, without a word being said, he handed me the sweater.

❖ Don't hide when you make mistakes

Once, I approached Guru with a problem that I had been carrying and working on for fifteen years. Only a few days earlier, he commented that he was pleased with my spiritual progress. Now, three days later, I broached the topic with him. "Guru, I still have this difficulty in life. I still think the wrong thoughts constantly."

His response was interesting. "Do you remember three days ago when I told you that I was pleased with you?"

"Yes," I said.

He added, "Good. Every time you have this wrong thought remember how pleased I am with you!"

I was surprised by his response. You see, this is just the opposite of how I was conditioned to feel all my life. Whenever I would witness these inappropriate thought-actions in my life, I would typically respond with some combination of militaristic-misery theater, ranging from "Oh, God, I've got to fix that; I've got to conquer that," to "I am unworthy, useless and hopeless." With these declarations, I felt that I was putting myself back on the right side of my aspiration.

Guru read the surprised and perhaps perplexed look on my face. "Yes, every time you have a wrong thought, think a good thought right afterwards. Use the right thought to cure a wrong thought." He added, "When you do something wrong, you run away from Light, from your Source. You want to hide and in so doing, you separate yourself from your Source. This will only increase the likelihood of you doing the wrong thing again. Instead, you should run towards Light. You should always include God in your actions, good or bad. In this way, you'll strengthen the good and illumine the bad."

❖ "I am a real tiger"

Back in the old days, there were Centres established in a number of Midwest cities, including Milwaukee, Ann Arbor, St. Louis and Kansas City. The members were all quite close. Unfortunately, the Centre leaders of one Midwest Centre were experiencing a marital problem which resulted in some inappropriate behavior on both the part of the husband and wife. I sent a report of this to Guru.

In 1974, Guru inititated a Fifty Oneness-State Run. He was planning to both run in each of the fifty U.S. states and give a talk in that state as well. As fate would have it, Guru was coming to Chicago just two weeks after I made my report to Guru.

Guru actually called me to find out the details of the situation. After informing him as best I could, he told me to ensure that the couple would come to Chicago where he would speak to them.

After Guru's morning run, Guru called the two of them over to him for a private interview. I was within earshot of this, as I was guarding Guru's privacy. Guru spoke to them so lovingly and with such compassion and concern. He was so gentle and wise in his counsel, after which the husband commented, "Guru, we have to admit that we were afraid and embarrassed to approach you about this."

With a sweet smile, Guru "blessingfully" looked at them and said, "Yes, I am a real tiger."

❖ "Just be happy"

When I had my first restaurant, I had the opportunity to approach Guru many times with the myriad problems I experienced while running the restaurant. Guru was always there to give me advice and counsel. One time, after about a half-hour's worth of talking, the final thing he said to me, in the sweetest and most reassuring voice, was, "Pradhan, good boy, just be happy and God will solve all your problems."

Now think about it. Is that the deal we seek to cut? No, I think it's just the opposite. We say, "God, just solve all my problems and I'll be happy." Guru's counsel was just in the reverse order! When we can create an inner environment of peace, poise, dignity and happiness, that environment allows the higher forces to operate through us, so we can better resolve our outer problems.

❖ Be careful what you say!

During the tenure of the first Victory's Banner Restaurant, 1981-86, I would attend all the Christmas trips, which lasted two to three weeks back then. Sukantika, my spiritual sister who served as manager of the restaurant, would work overtime to cover my absence, so whenever Guru took his smaller European trips during the year, I would make an effort to send Sukantika.

Although the restaurant was always financially strapped, one year we were really hurting and didn't have enough funds to send Sukantika on the mid-year European journey. I felt badly about this, and one day approached Guru on his porch, explaining that we didn't have enough money and asking if it was absolutely necessary to send Sukantika. He said, "It is all a matter of consciousness. If her consciousness is going to fall, then she should definitely go. Consciousness comes before money."

"Okay," I replied, "I'll tell her that."

"Oh no, don't tell her that!" Guru clarified. "Tell her that if she can keep her same good consciousness as it is and not go, then she doesn't have to go." Then he clarified, "The very suggestion that her consciousness may go down will serve as a seed to cause it to go down. Always say things in such a way as to inspire people, not discourage them." It struck me how careful Guru is, down to the last word.

❖ Guru's 50th birthday nap

For Guru's 50th birthday, the first incarnation of Victory's Banner was in full swing, and we were given the honor of preparing and serving dinner for this special birthday. Because it was special, we suggested, and Guru agreed, to have a sit-down dinner with waiter service! Our sister restaurant in San Francisco was very helpful to Victory's Banner in its opening days, and so they joined us in oneness. On the evening of August 26th, I went to check out the kitchen facilities at the school in Connecticut where the event was to be held.

Three years earlier, Guru spontaneously asked of his students, "Who will run 47 miles on my birthday?" As a Centre, our running had progressed to the point of exploring ultra-marathons. With this simple question from Guru, the annual 47-mile race was born. Each year it began at midnight of Guru's birthday.

For this 50th birthday, the race was extended to 50 miles! After checking out the dining and kitchen facilities, I arrived at the race site at about 1 a.m. The race was being held in a park in Nyack, NY, just across the Tappan Zee Bridge. It was a warm, beautiful evening (now early morning).

At seeing me, Guru called me over to check if everything was all right. I was anticipating staying up all night to help with the race, but Guru suggested something else. Knowing that the next day would be intensely busy for me, Guru told me to take a blanket and lie down to rest for a while within 10 feet of him, and then go home for a good night's rest. I had a delightful outdoor nap!

❖ Be a weightlifter

Whenever I visited Guru in New York, it was usually an escape from my responsibilities in Chicago. With that escape came more opportunity to meditate and maintain what appeared to be better spiritual discipline. Therefore, I was surprised when Guru told me that when I am in Chicago I make more progress. This was exactly contrary to my perceptions. So I said, "Guru, you know, I don't see it. You say I make more spiritual progress back in Chicago. I don't feel spiritual progress in Chicago. I feel nothing but struggle, nothing but difficulty."

Guru-isms

And he said, "No, no, no, it's not like that. Think of the weightlifter. The weightlifter lifts weights. Now, you can take all the weight off the barbell and the weightlifter says, 'Oh, look how easy it is for me. I can lift the weight so many times.' Now, put weights on the barbell. Immediately he will see it is much more difficult to lift. But in which way is he developing more strength? When the barbell has weights, of course." He added, "True, it is more difficult to lift. But at the same time, he is developing more strength. In life, what are your weights? Nothing other than your life's responsibilities, or you can call it your duties. Your life's responsibilities are the weights. So when you go back to Chicago, you assume your life's responsibilities, and it is these responsibilities that compel you to develop inner strength."

Sometimes there's a delicate balance between what we deem to be life-struggles and what truly are our proper life-opportunities. Life is constantly challenging us with the opportunity for self-transcendence.

9

Scoldings

There was no greater catalyst for change than one of Guru's scoldings. Period.[1]

❖ On scoldings

Scoldings came in various forms, from the mild to the severe. The mild ones were usually quite easy to take. Usually, they were greeted with folded hands, a serious face and a regular "Yes, Guru…yes, Guru…yes, Guru," and then you moved on. For example, one day during a multi-day race in New York where I was in charge of medical, I remember thinking that we did not have enough pictures of Guru in the medical tent. (I put these pictures up to provide inspiration for both the runners and the medical staff.) As fate would have it, Guru inspected the area that day.

---

[1] Guru told me many times that this chapter was his favorite!

Scoldings

That night, Guru called me over to his home and said in a mildly scolding tone, "How is it that you do not have pictures up in the medical tent?"

This was an easy one because I had just seen the problem myself. "Yes, Guru, of course Guru, I'll correct it, Guru," I replied, and then I smiled.

Guru said to Pulak who was standing nearby, "Pulak, now that I've scolded Pradhan, I feel much better, much better." Then to me, "Now come and massage me."

The more serious scoldings should be greeted with the same affirmation-joy-acceptance but, for me at least, that was not the case. First of all, these scoldings were quite difficult to endure. Often, because you didn't want to be wrong, your ego came to the fore with a number of "but Guru's" which were said in private conversation to yourself—although I have witnessed some of my brothers "but Guru-ing" right in front of Guru.

Having received many of these scoldings, I can testify that Guru's scoldings were <u>never</u> wrong. In most cases, they came after years of Guru using his love and compassion to guide you in the direction you needed to go. If, after a few years, you did not honor Guru's advice, Guru used his justice-power. This was his job—your perfection.

Occasionally, there was a scolding that seemed to come out of the blue. For example, I have been scolded for things that other people had done wrong and I had no knowledge of their transgression whatsoever. At first glance, this may seem unfair, but it is not. In these cases, either (1) I should have known about their action, or (2) they acted because I relinquished my proper responsibility. Frankly, even if a scolding seemed completely unjustified at the time, the fact is, Guru could have justifiably scolded me virtually every day of my spiritual career. I could easily have received one of these seemingly unjustified scoldings just to make up for lost opportunities.

(Allow me a paranthetical comment: In the course of spiritual processing, in the Guru/student relationship, students often de-

Scoldings

ceive themselves quite a bit. The Guru and the student are both aware of the student's imperfections. But then, in the course of receiving affection and love from the Guru, we misintepret the Guru's tolerance for endorsement. The student then tolerates and even indulges his imperfections thinking, "Well, if Guru doesn't mind them." Wrong. Totally wrong. In my life, Guru was the only one who wanted my perfection completely, totally and unconditionally. His scoldings were a reflection of that. Often I heard him say, "Would I scold a dog in the street? I scold you because I love you and care for your perfection.")

The worst scoldings, the "ruthless" ones as Guru himself might refer to them, were painful to hear, but they forced you to change like nothing else. Unlike the scolding we all may have received from a parent or school teacher, these scoldings reached way down into the inner being. Let me share with you the experience. Imagine that you are having open heart surgery—without any anesthetic. Your chest is wide open, your heart fully exposed. Then along comes the scolding message on a red hot branding iron, and it is emblazoned on your heart. You heal, but the message is permanently imprinted on the tablet of your heart. Sounds scary, yes? Honestly, yes...the experience is tough, but it is as though you are being force-fed a profound spiritual Truth that is essential for your progress. (Eat your spiritual spinach! It's good for you!)

I think Guru would have preferred not to use this tool if it were not necessary. We do not need to make mistakes in order to learn a lesson. We can learn by virtue of our faith-obedience just as well. For example, a mother might tell her child not to touch the flame on the stove or he will get burned. The child could simply trust his mother and learn this lesson without ever testing it. Alternatively, if the child is mischievous, he may in fact touch the stove and get burned, at which time the mother says with raised voice, "I told you not to touch the stove! Why didn't you listen to me?!" The wrong action invoked a scolding from the mother re-

Scoldings

sulting in a double punishment—the child was both burned and scolded. The lesson is learned, but in this case with more pain.

This is our choice as students. The Guru wants to guide us to our perfection-life. We can choose to simply listen, be obedient, and by virtue of faith-obedience, learn the lessons we need. Or, we can be disobedient and get burned. We arrive at the same place, but the latter path is more painful. In the spiritual life, our mischief—disobedience in all of its various forms—is much more dangerous than touching the stove. Indeed, disobedience can prove fatal to our spiritual lives. In this regard, Guru's scoldings were our surest protection and safety.

Although part of me feared receiving them, let me say that I loved Guru's scoldings, and in hindsight I am so grateful that he blessed me with them. They intensified my meditation and accelerated my progress like nothing else. There were actually times when I prayed for the capacity to receive one scolding a day.

In fact, late in Guru's life, Guru himself seemed to have taken some joy and pride in the scoldings he had given me over the years, and in the fact that I endured them. Many years ago he told me that my best quality was that no matter how many times I fall, I pick myself up, dust myself off, and start walking again towards the goal. In 2004, I received a wonderful experience in the form of a message from Guru.

It was the occasion of my birthday and I wanted to offer prasad at Guru's home. That year, my birthday fell on the same day as the birthday celebration for Guru's beloved sister Lily, and because of those festivities, I felt it was especially important to seek Guru's permission to offer prasad. This was confirmed by my spiritual sister Shephali, who turned out to be the messenger in this case.

On my behalf, she asked Guru if I could bring prasad. With a stern voice, Guru replied "NO! Tell him Sandy is a much better student than Pradhan! Tell him I don't need his prasad!" Then with utmost affection he said, "Oy, I have so much love and affection for him, does he have to ask this kind of question? Tell him, 'He is my compassion-affection-proof, insult-proof, ruthless scolding-proof student.' " Then he added, "Still, Sandy is a much better student than Pradhan. At least now he knows I remember his old name!"

In sharing my scoldings in this little booklet, I will spare you the details which brought Guru to the point of scolding me. Rather, it is Guru's methods, his love and affection I hope to convey.

Thank you, Guru, a million times, thank you, Guru.

❖ One million lifetimes

Although this hardly qualifies as a scolding, I place it here because it came just two weeks after the experience I wrote about above. It seemed to be a continuation of sorts.

I was called to Guru's home to work on his knee, which had become significantly more painful. In a rather stern and tough voice Guru told me, "Good boy, do a good job, do a good job. You have to cure me. Otherwise, I'll fire you and take away your name. I will call you Sandy again." Then his voice became absolutely soft, sweet and loving. Seemingly enjoying his own toughness, he added, "It will take you one million lifetimes to realize how much love I have for you."

❖ My first scolding

I believe it was 1979 when I received my first serious scolding. It was exactly two days before Guru was to come to Chicago for the Sri Chinmoy Tennis Tournament, the very first event of its kind. My good friend and fellow Chicago student Anugata was the premier tennis player in the Centre at that time. He had professional capacities in every way and organized this tournament for girls aged fourteen years and under.

I was in a good consciousness and was anticipating Guru's visit with a great deal of joy and excitement. Two days before his visit, however, came a very surprising and painful phone call. It was

Scoldings

Ashrita. "Guru said he is extremely disappointed in you. How could you have done such a thing? How could you have said what you did? I will never allow you to be close to me for doing this kind of thing!"

I was shocked and apologetic from the depth of my heart. I immediately wrote Guru a note begging his forgiveness for whatever I had done. But, I had no idea what it was that I had done wrong! The following day, I received a message back that Guru forgave me.

Well, this certainly changed my inner attitude about Guru's visit. I was tentative and prepared myself for Guru's illumination-scolding.

The entire Centre was there to greet Guru at the airport. Guru got in the car and invited Anugata to come with us, since he was the organizer of the tournament. We drove to the location and dropped Anugata off and proceeded to Guru's hotel. At long last, I was with Guru alone. Guru was playing his flute.

"All right Guru, I am ready for your blessing-scolding."

"What scolding?" Guru replied.

"Well Guru, just two days ago—perhaps you don't recall—but you scolded me quite nicely."

"Oh that. The past is dust, the past is dust." Guru went on playing his flute.

"But Guru, the thing is, I have absolutely no idea what it was that I did!"

Then Guru went on to explain. It had to do with something that I did a year or two earlier that he had just found out about! After listening to Guru's words, I realized my error, but more than that—the incredible wisdom that was present in Guru's words. He told me that with everything that I do, I must look at the implication of my actions three, four or five steps down the road. Based on my past transgression, so many problems could have been created for myself and for him. Fortunately, they did not manifest, but they could have.

The subtler lesson here was that we cannot escape the consequences of our actions. Here I was being scolded for something that happened more than a year earlier! When we do the wrong thing, the forces of correction must operate for our own sake. Our perfection is Guru's responsibility and the Supreme's necessity, so how can it be otherwise? There is no such thing as "getting away with something," even if that thing was done unconsciously.

❖ "You will get your realization from this"

In 1979, I requested and received an interview with Guru. It was an important interview, because I confessed to Guru that I was having a problem in my spiritual life, which I felt was "spiritually life-threatening." Guru listened and affirmed my assessment. Guru very lovingly counseled me on the necessary attitudes and actions to right the situation.

Over the next three years or so, I dealt with this situation, more or less—sometimes more—more often less, but I never fully implemented Guru's guidance. Although one could easily make excuses such as, "Oh it was difficult," "Oh I tried but," and so on. The root of this failure was that I did not *want* to follow Guru's guidance.

This is an example of what I spoke of earlier—I fooled myself into thinking that Guru's tolerance of a situation was the same as Guru's acceptance and even approval.

One morning, I walked into the first incarnation of Victory's Banner Restaurant and commented to a co-worker that I felt really strange that morning. "It feels as if my heart has been torn out of my being," I said. These were my precise words. These were unusual words, but an even more unusual experience. These words proved to be quite prophetic.

Within five minutes the phone rang. It was Ashrita. "Guru said you have to leave the path. For three years now you have not listened to him, and now he can no longer accept it. You have to leave."

Scoldings

I was devastated and immediately broke down, "I will listen, I promise, I promise. Please, I beg Guru, ask Guru to please forgive me." I was in tears. I felt badly for Ashrita, who is my friend, and had to play this role. "Okay, I'll give him your message," he said.

A situation of this sort usually gets Guru's prompt attention. He wants to know your responses and reactions. I sat downstairs in the restaurant office in tears and the phone rang. "Guru said 'No'," came Ashrita's voice. "It is too late."

Now I was crying openly. "Please Ashrita, ask Guru if I can move back to New York. I will be the tiniest ant in his family if he'll allow me to stay. Please, ask Guru."

"I don't think it will matter," replied Ashrita, "but if he calls, I'll ask."

Five minutes passed that seemed like an hour. The phone rang. "No, you have to leave the path."

I was now resigned to my fate. "What would Guru have me do with the restaurant? Shall I give it to the girls?" (There were two girls who managed the restaurant.)

Minutes later the phone rang. "Fine, you can give it to the girls if you want, or you can do whatever you want with it."

I sat and cried and cried and sat. There was nothing else to do. Tears streamed down my cheeks nonstop. I called my brother Lenny in California to ask if he could house me for a while. I told him what was happening. He was very kind in extending his sympathy to me. I affirmed to him that Guru was absolutely right in taking this action, that Guru had been more than patient. The next call was to United Airlines to arrange a flight.

I took a music book and a little portable keyboard instrument, and left with just that. My brother lives right near the redwoods of Marin County, California. It was my intention to first go to his home, and then to get lost in the woods quietly playing Guru's music until I died. I said my "goodbyes" and left requesting that Sukantika "Tell Madhava (who was and remains a dear friend) that I love him."

Scoldings

I must have looked a mess when I arrived at O'Hare Airport. The flight attendant at the United desk looked at me and said, "Sir, I'm going to clear an entire aisle for you so you can lie down and rest. Something serious has happened, hasn't it?"

I took off my glasses to cover my eyes in embarrassment. I saw how she knew. My glasses were completely coated with the salt of dried tears. "Yes, something serious," I said, and thanked her for her consideration.

For the duration of the four-hour flight, I lay down across the empty row of seats painfully chanting to myself, "Supreme, forgive me…Guru, forgive me…Supreme, forgive me…Guru forgive me." For four long hours, no other thought occupied my being.

When I arrived in San Francisco, Lenny greeted me at the gate with a hug and a sad face. "I have to call the restaurant," I told him. "It feels as if my heart is back."

I called the restaurant. Sukantika answered. Excitedly she said, "Call New York right away. Ashrita's been trying to get a hold of you." There was a painful hope in my heart.

This was before the days of cell phones. I had no coins, and credit cards could not be used with phones, so I had to make a collect call through the operator. The line was busy, but the operator could detect something in my voice. "Is this a matter of life and death?" she asked.

"Yes," was my only response.

"I'll break into the line for you." She broke into Ashrita's call and I could hear her talking. "There is a Mr. Balter on the line with an emergency call. Can I interrupt this call for you to take it?" And then to me she said, "Please hold the line."

Ashrita's voice came on the phone, "Pradhan, Guru said he forgives you, he forgives you! We tried to stop the plane. Even after it left the gate, we tried to get them to get you off the plane, but they wouldn't do it."

There was more to the message. "Guru said to spend a few days with your brother and then to come to New York." More importantly, along with the message came a specific set of instruc-

Scoldings

tions that I had to follow. They were strict instructions and they required an immediate and difficult change in me.

A few days later I arrived in New York, and as soon as Guru was informed of my arrival, I was called to his home. I was sitting alone on the front porch when Guru came out, sat down, meditated with me and then said, "You will get your realization from this."

I had written Guru a note and asked if he had read it.

"No," he said, "what did it say?"

I began to explain, "Guru, I offered an alternative plan."

"Stop!" Guru cut me off mid-sentence. Then in a very loving tone he said, "Let me explain what happened in your case. Early in the morning I was sitting in the living room, practicing my music, when the Supreme appeared before me and said, 'Tell Pradhan this.' So I gave you the message. Later in the day, the Supreme appeared before me again and said, 'All right. Pradhan's heart has come to the fore. Tell him you forgive him and give him this message.' So, here the Supreme appears before me and tells me exactly what I am supposed to say to you, and now you come to me with a different plan? Just who I am supposed to listen to, you or the Supreme?

"Your sole responsibility is to listen to me. The moment you don't listen to me and listen instead to your unillumined mind or emotional life, you are taking the first step out of my boat and into your own boat."

During this time, I sat with folded hands, listening. There was such compassion and affection in Guru's voice as he was saying this. For the next few days, while I was in New York, Guru had me at his feet as much as possible. While it appeared as though I was massaging him, in fact, he was massaging me with his compassion and affection.

It also struck me that you can never rely on appearances. Here I was on Guru's left side, his right side and at his feet. One could have easily concluded, "Oh how close he is." But in reality, only a few days earlier I had brought Guru to the point where he was compelled to ask me to leave.

Thirty-nine years after being accepted by Guru, I can say with absolute certainty that it was 100 percent by Guru's forgiveness-patience-love-tolerance that I was allowed to remain with him.

It was all his grace—all his grace.

❖ The three-month "vacation"

In 1997, Guru visited a Centre where he saw someone in attendance that he had never formally accepted as a student. The explanation for this was that their picture was submitted, but no response was ever received, so it was simply assumed that the person was accepted. As you might expect, Guru was quite upset over this and the inquiry then went out to all the Centres whether or not any Centre leader had allowed a non-student to attend the regular Centre meetings?

When it came time for Ashrita to ask me, I reminded him that 20 to 25 years ago, this was quite common place. In fact, we even brought people to New York before they were formally accepted by Guru as students. Furthermore, although I couldn't give a specific instance when I allowed someone to come, I'm sure I did, or at least would have. (Later, I remembered many now prominent students who were in this boat!) Well, that was enough to fit the criteria and the appropriate justice was meted out to me and all of those Centre leaders who did this: a three-month "vacation". Furthermore, Guru said that we could not participate in any Centre activity, but that students could and should be nice to us and talk with us.

Almost all of the Centre leaders in the U.S. and Australia fit the bill and the vacation was given to all of us.

It was an interesting experience, to say the least. Since we were allowed to speak with each other, the first thing I did was to call all my fellow Centre leaders. I must confess that I was surprised by the response of some of them. Some were in tears, oth-

Scoldings

ers traumatized. I suggested, "Hey, this is Guru's game. He knows what he is doing." I also felt there might be more here than met the eye. My personal opinion was that Guru wanted to shake things up, but it is not really necessary to seek another motive to appreciate what took place over the next three months.

The vacation was an interesting experience because outwardly there was the sense that you were on your own. It differed from when someone left or was asked to leave the path, because I believe Guru was more inwardly present in a vacation. I felt like he was hiding on the sidelines, watching and protecting to make sure you didn't get too lost. I operated under the illusion that I had some base level of spirituality that was mine. After all, I meditated everyday.

And so the vacation began. I must confess that part of me was happy and relieved to be free of the responsibility of the Centre leadership. I was true to Guru's instruction. Since I lived at the Centre, I would meditate before everyone came for Centre meditation. Before they arrived, I would leave the Centre, returning again when the meditation was over and all had left. Although other students were given the okay to be in touch with us, I hardly heard from anyone, which saddened me a bit. I would talk to Ashrita with some regularity.

I was surprised that some Centre leaders called almost daily to ask permission to do this or do that. I remember thinking to myself, "God, if we can't be obedient when Guru says to do nothing, how can we be obedient when Guru says to do something?" Others meditated with seekers from other paths just to be in touch with aspiration. This drew a ripe chastising from Guru.

For me, I was ignorantly happy in my do-nothing mode. Slowly and steadily I witnessed my so-called base-level aspiration erode. My meditations became shorter and shorter. On Wednesday evenings, when I would leave the Centre, I would usually find myself in a café. In the beginning, simple socializing with the coffee drinker at the next table would lead to a talk on the spiritual life–led by me. Over time, however, this phenomenon disap-

Scoldings

peared and as more time passed, I even felt at a loss for words. If you knew me, you'd equate this with a miracle.

At one point about midway through the three months, Guru offered a public meditation. Afterwards, he questioned why those on vacation did not come. With one voice, we responded that we did not know we were allowed to come.

Ashrita sent the message that on a certain date Guru was holding another public event and he said the people in "jail" (this was a humorous and affectionate description) could all come, but by now, I was well settled in my "Guru said to do nothing so I'm doing nothing" mode. Everyone went except one person—me. That evening Guru called all the vacationers to him and meditated with them. Although I was not there, I didn't hear anything from Guru about it.

As the second month of my vacation experience came and passed, my aspiration had all but disappeared. I wasn't meditating well, or for any significant length of time. Furthermore, for a member of any Centre there are any number of duties that have to be performed… postering for classes, singing practices, etc. When you are in a good consciousness, these kinds of things are done with a joyful willingness, but there are often times when they are performed because it is simply what is expected of you. This is particularly true as a Centre leader, because everyone is looking to you to set an example. Well, all of these things were gone from me now, even the services done reluctantly. I can tell you now that a service or duty reluctantly performed is better than no service at all. The Centre and its associated duties serve as a support mechanism for your own aspiration.

The three-month vacation, in theory, extended through Guru's Birthday Celebration. The vacationers were all informed that we could come for the celebrations for two weeks from August 17th through the 30th. I had made my reservations for August 17th. Then word came from Guru that we could come August 15th because there was going to be a special celebration for the 50th anniversary of India's independence. For me, that meant changing

Scoldings

my reservation and incurring about $200 in additional flight fees, which I was reluctant to spend. Then, about five days later came the message that we could all come in on the 13th for some other reason. Well, that was it. I decided not to change my initial reservation at all and come on the evening of the 17th, as originally planned.

As the day approached, slowly, steadily and unerringly, I witnessed my aspiration and inspiration degenerate. As August arrived, I felt I had absolutely nothing left, and that I was nothing. I remember speaking to my dear friend Sunil during the first week of August, telling him that I was basically coming to Celebrations to say "goodbye" to everyone including Guru—that aspiration was dead in me. This was really how I felt, and I thought it to be my genuine intention.

I arrived late on the evening of the 17th, showered and went to the function. The end of evening prasad was just being taken, so I got in line and when the time came, took my prasad, turned to Guru and bowed. He definitely looked at me, but I was spared the chiding I fully expected. Every other vacationer had arrived days earlier. I deserved a scolding for my attitude and lack of aspiration, but didn't get one. I was sure that I had actually gone beyond the point of redemption. Why should Guru bother to scold me?

The evening of the next day I got a phone call with a message. "Guru said to come to his house right away to massage him. Bring the table." (The table refers to the massage table which resides in Guru's home.) I was surprised. I showered and off I went. Oh God, I must confess that I was dreading this. You see, whenever I went to New York, I stood in front of Guru at the first opportunity and inwardly purged myself of everything I had done wrong and accumulated since my last visit. Then I smiled, literally. I've learned the value of this over the years. It was a waste of time to put on misery theatrics in front of Guru. It didn't help in any way whatsoever in your progress life.

Scoldings

This was not, however, my typical visit to New York. I had not seen Guru in three months. Although in New York, I was still officially on vacation. I had made no sincere effort to see him when the opportunity was offered. I came late to Celebrations. And last but not least, my life of aspiration was non-existent.

When I arrived at Guru's home, despite his specific request, I went to the basement and stayed there. I did not have the courage to face Guru. I sat and prayed and decided to stay put until I heard, "Oy, where is he?", which I knew would be forthcoming.

"Oy, where is he?" took about three minutes to come. I braced myself and carried the table up the stairs and out to the porch where Guru was lying on his sofa. My head was bowed and I walked in like a dog with his tail between his legs.

Upon seeing me, "Come good boy, tonight you are out of jail. Please come to my house every night to massage me. You don't have to be informed." That was it. No scolding, no chiding, no anything in reference to my state of being. Guru was his loving self. We chatted and chatted some more, and laughed a bit. I felt again a familiar joy that had left me.

A few days later, something significant happened. For the first time in what seemed ages, I had the thought "My consciousness is not where it should be. I have to meditate." Oh my God! An aspiring thought!!!

And with that thought came an inner experience. Guru was reborn in me. I saw that without Guru, I quickly eroded to nothing. Remember that base aspiration that I assumed was mine? Well, there is no base aspiration. In fact, Guru was present in and is responsible for even the most basic, simplest, aspiration-thought. Without him, there is no Pradhan, no meditation, no spiritual life. Someday, I hope to develop the gratitude that he deserves.

❖ **The 3-elevator stop scolding (part 1):**
Guru's words can burn your heart

It was in the Bahamas, and I was enjoying a delightful outer relationship with Guru, one that I was putting at risk by virtue of my

Scoldings

not listening to a specific command-request from Guru. This is another case of disciple-delusion, where we misinterpret Guru's outer attention-fondness with his acceptance-tolerance of our misdeeds. Mistake.

I had just completed massaging duties, when Ashrita broached me with a question, "Is it true that you did 'such and such.'" "Yes, it's true," I said. I knew I was in for a huge and well-deserved scolding and Guru did not disappoint me. Guru was absolutely disgusted and he let me know it, not once, but regularly over the next three to four days. All of these scolding-messages came via Ashrita. I was not getting anything directly from Guru himself. Once again, I felt sorry for Ashrita because, besides being Guru's message-giver, he is also my good friend and I felt his identification with me as well as his obedience to Guru.

Of course, somehow, some way, all this was to be taken with a smile. Guru's scoldings were for our illumination. Nevertheless, this was not an easy task. I also knew that if Guru were to get me alone, I would hear it directly from him, which would be even more painful. I was not prepared for that, so as much as possible, I avoided direct interaction with Guru. For example, I would either not take prasad, or sneak up in a crowd. I would always sit in the last row of the function hall, making myself as invisible as possible.

The most difficult avoidance was the elevator. You see, in this particular hotel for some strange reason, many boys were actually put in rooms one floor above Guru's room. This is a most unusual arrangement. Almost always Guru is on a top floor, which is as it should be, but in this case, I and many others were on the 7th floor, while Guru's room was on the 6th floor. So, to avoid any possibility of running into Guru one-on-one, I never took the elevator. I walked up and down all seven floors every time I had to exit the hotel. I was successful—until the last day.

On the last day, because I was carrying my suitcases, I had no choice but to take the elevator. I got on the 7th floor praying it would go all the way down, but I should have known better. The elevator stopped on the 6th floor, opened, and there was Guru. Yes, Guru walked in and he and I were alone on the elevator, and the first-hand scolding began. Oh my God, Guru was justifiably relentless. "You have been with me 30 years. You have wasted my time; I have wasted your time. Someday, you will realize who I am…you will take me as your spiritual Master and listen to me. But now, we are just wasting each other's time."

I can assure you, this is a very watered down version of what took place. In fact, this scolding started on the 6th floor, went down to the lobby where the door opened. I was standing in the corner of the elevator with Guru scolding me in loud tones when the door opened. I suspect there were students there looking in, but all they could see was Guru, as I was squeezing myself into a corner. The elevator door closed and reopened on the 2nd floor. As Guru was concentrating only on one thing, he was oblivious to the openings of the elevator and he began to exit the 2nd floor. I followed him, meekly interjecting that we were on the wrong floor. The scolding then continued from the 2nd floor back to the lobby where Guru finally exited and I followed. About 10 feet outside the elevator door, it ended.

I was devastated, totally devastated—beyond devastation, in fact. And I deserved every word of it.

(As an aside, being a recipient of many of Guru's "ruthless" scoldings, whenever you received one, you felt it couldn't get any worse. Well, this is not true. Guru applied his principles of transcendence even in his scolding world, and each worse possible scolding was transcended by the next one, making its predecessor a mere puppy!)

At any rate, this scolding left me in absolute ashes. We were on our way to the airport. There I found Ashrita. Since he had already been in the midst of this, I told him what had happened in this last chapter and that it was too much for me to bear. I informed him that I would be going home as there was no sense to be on the Christmas trip. I emphasized that I was not leaving the path, but simply that I would be better off working than being on

Scoldings

the trip. I asked him where I could catch a flight home. He directed me to the next terminal, but also told me that he would tell Guru what I was doing.

I made my way over to the nearby terminal from where I could catch a flight back to the U.S., and hid in some remote corner, huddled in a vertical fetal position while tears slowly streamed down my cheeks.

A few minutes later I heard Guru's voice as he was walking towards me, "Oy, where is he, where is he?," upon which the slow stream of tears became a flood, and I hid my face saying, "I am sorry, I am sorry." At seeing me, Guru said not to go home and to come on the trip. He said, "All right, I forgive you, I forgive you. Would I bark at a dog on the street? No. I scold you because I love you."

"Guru," I said, "I was enjoying such a sweet outer relationship with you, and now I've ruined it. I don't feel I can look at you." By this I meant that I did not deserve to look at Guru.

Guru quickly said, "Look at me, look at me," which I forced myself to do, and he was beaming with his transcendent eyes and a beautiful smile. "Now come," he said.

I gathered myself and followed. Upon returning to the group, people noticed my red eyes. "Severe allergy attack," I told them.

❖ **The 3-elevator stop scolding (part 2):**
Guru's words can melt your heart

In the weeks that followed, I smiled as best I could, but inwardly was still allowing the wounds to heal. Additionally, I didn't really feel that I deserved Guru's forgiveness—that I had forced his hand. At functions, I continued my habit of sitting way in the back, making myself as small as possible.

This trip had taken us from the Bahamas to Guatamala and finally to Mexico. We were now in Merida, Mexico, perhaps some five weeks into our journey when the phone rang. "Pradhan? Guru wants to speak with you" came the message.

Scoldings

"Pradhan," Guru said. "How is it that I am not seeing you at the functions?"

"Guru, I have been there, but I have been sitting in the back. But I have been there."

"But why are you not sitting in the front? A significant disciple like you should be sitting in the front," Guru replied with a bit of a smile in his voice.

"Well, Guru, I really haven't felt like I should be sitting in the front," I said.

"But I told you that I forgave you, didn't I?" Guru asked.

"Yes, Guru, but I sort of felt that I forced your hand and that I didn't really deserve your forgiveness."

Then the heart melting began. Guru asked tenderly, "Did I do the wrong thing in scolding you?"

"No, Guru," I replied, "You were perfectly right in scolding me. I did the wrong thing."

Then Guru completely disarmed me. So sweetly Guru said, "Oy, but I have ruined your entire vacation!"

Guru was just killing me with affection. "Now, you come downstairs and massage me."

Guru's earlier words burned me to a crisp. Now his words were melting my heart.

❖ The student's oneness

There has never been a time after receiving a personal public scolding when I was not approached by any number of my brother/sister students saying, "You know, that scolding was really for me." This is how it should be for any number of reasons. For one thing, none of us is absent of imperfection, so when I was scolded for a particular flaw in my character or behavior, others have that flaw also. On another level, there is (as there should be) some degree of oneness amongst the students, so simply by virtue of identification, every scolding could be taken personally by everyone. I certainly felt this when others got Guru's "special blessings", as he often called them!

Scoldings

It is a very important aspect of the Guru-student relationship that the student identifies with the Guru's consciousness to such an extent that he actually sees the world through his Guru's eyes. Guru was fond of telling two stories, one about Ramakrishna and one about Krishna. In the first case, Ramakrishna was with two of his disciples and all of them had not eaten and were quite hungry. There was only a morsel of food available, which the disciples happily offered to their Master, who ate the food. However, their identification with Ramakrishna was so complete, that when Ramakrishna ate the food, the two disciples with him felt their hunger satisfied.

The Krishna story Guru told even more often. Krishna was travelling with his dearest devotee, Arjuna. Krishna described a tree, seeing it as black. Arjuna affirmed, "Yes, it is black." Then immediately Krishna said the tree was green. Arjuna again affirmed, "Yes, the tree is green." Guru explained that this was not merely blind surrender, but in fact, Arjuna was so immersed in Krishna's consciousness that he was actually seeing the tree through Krishna's eyes.

This identification in consciousness is the key ingredient in the Guru-student relationship. As such, it is inappropriate for a student to argue with his Teacher, unless the Teacher himself invites the discussion. Certainly this is true when receiving a "special blessing"! I have learned that the best way to receive a scolding is to simply smile and go into absorption mode.

One time, while visiting New York with some of my Chicago brothers and sisters, we Chicagoans were given the opportunity to sing a few spiritual songs. But before we started, Guru very nicely offered a "special blessing" to me. It was a mild scolding, and one which I could easily absorb and agree with, so there was no resistance on my part in receiving it. Shortly thereafter, Guru invited everyone to participate in a "walk-past". During a walk-past, Guru entered into a very high meditation, as each student walked meditatively past him for a moment's blessing. As I approached Guru, I was so happy to see him that a broad smile came over my face. Guru immediately grabbed the microphone. I remember thinking "Uh oh, here comes more scolding!" But no—Guru said, "There is nothing that gives me more joy or makes me more proud than to see someone smile when I give him a scolding. This is the disciple's absolute oneness with his Guru." And while my name was not mentioned, I knew Guru was responding to the fact that I was smiling so broadly at seeing him.

Depending on the intensity of the scolding and one's own surrender, the "smiling-absorption" mode was not always easy and required a sublimation of the ego's natural inclination to defend oneself, that is, to prove oneself right. But this sublimation is precisely what the disciple is attempting to do in his own spiritual quest, and a scolding often forced the issue!

I think it is true that we invest a lot of time in this kind of activity, that is, defending our own particular perspective on things. On a human level, it validates us, but it is not necessarily a divine quality at all. Until we realize the highest Truth, we live in a world of only relative truth. It is an excellent exercise to practice humility, and when confronted with a perspective that is different from your own, to simply remain silent and accept.

And certainly, when you have a spiritual Teacher, your responsibility is to accept the Teacher's direction to you as coming from your own inner being. You do not argue with your Master; although, God bless my brothers and sisters, I have witnessed quite a few of them doing so! And inwardly, I confess—I have done my share, especially as you'll see in the next story.

❖ **China**
   The scolding to end all scoldings
   Let me forewarn you—as a reader, you may find yourself wondering how and why this happened the way it did. This scolding was the most painful experience of my "scolding career," so please allow me to prepare you. As you first read this, you may think that the pain came from the fact that I was scolded so publicly and for something that was slightly misrepresented to Guru.

Scoldings

But no, that is not the case. The pain came from my own response to the scolding, which was inappropriate, and perhaps was the real reason I received this scolding in the first place!

First of all, if you have not already done so, please read *The student's oneness* on page 111 in which I write about the necessity to identify with the Guru's consciousness, and that arguing a point is always inappropriate. Sometimes the Teacher will do something which may be deliberately painful and difficult to endure, but it serves an ultimate good. In this regard, I am reminded of two stories—the first, a movie plot and the second, a more poignant story about a great Tibetan yogi.

The movie is more light-hearted. In the movie *The Karate Kid*, young Daniel wants to learn Karate from his teacher, Mr. Miyagi. What does Mr. Miyagi teach him? First he teaches him to "wax the car," then "sand the floor," and finally "paint the house". All this time, unbeknownst to young Daniel, while he is performing these seemingly trivial tasks, he is learning and repeating the very movements he requires to master his Karate. While perhaps a bit trite, the lesson holds true that often the Teacher will put the student through an experience which the student himself doesn't understand at the time. But, when at last the lesson is learned, the experience seems to be all worthwhile.

The second story is far more significant. One of my favorite narratives is that found in the book *Milarepa—Tibet's greatest Yogi* by J. Evans Wentz. Milarepa was born to a well-to-do and most generous father and inherited his father's estate when his father passed away. However, because he was not of age, his father temporarily gave responsibility of the estate to Milarepa's maternal aunt and uncle until Milarepa turned 18. But instead of playing the role of caretakers to the estate, the aunt and uncle claimed the estate as their own and enslaved Milarepa and his mother.

Milarepa's mother was scarred beyond repair and it was at her behest that Milarepa studied and mastered "the dark arts" to wreak revenge on his aunt and uncle. He was quite successful in

Scoldings

his revenge, killing some 18 people and keeping the townspeople who sided with his aunt and uncle in a constant state of fear.

Milarepa, however, was filled with remorse for his actions and, with the blessings of his dark arts Master, sought to undo his wrong deeds by dedicating himself to a genuine spiritual Teacher and path. His Teacher was a great Yogi named Marpa, who promised to initiate Milarepa as soon as Milarepa completed one simple task–to build a small home of stone for Marpa and his wife. Well, Marpa seemingly puts Milarepa through a living hell of work, humiliation and then more work and humiliation as he makes Milarepa build, then tear down and then build again house after house, promising initiation with the completion of each. All this time, it appears that Marpa is cruel beyond belief. Often appearing drunk or insane, he would beat Milarepa, sometimes physically, sometimes emotionally and psychically.

Only at the very end is it revealed that Marpa was doing whatever was necessary to relieve Milarepa of the terrible karmic consequences of his dark art misdeeds. Because of Marpa's seeming brutality, Milarepa actually goes on to become Tibet's greatest yogi. And, what appeared to be insensitivity on the part of Marpa, was in reality Marpa's wisdom and compassion. He saw Milarepa's capacity and did whatever was necessary for Milarepa to make absolutely the fastest progress.

Indeed, this is the rightful role of every genuine Master. He has no other purpose than this. And in this regard, Guru proved himself again and again to me. He was the only one who stood absolutely for my God-realization and nothing else.

The story of Milarepa is an incredibly inspiring story about one man's intense aspiration for the highest Truth. In a single lifetime, Milarepa goes from the lowest to the highest. It is also an extreme example of how the Teacher's actions at first appearance can be terribly misunderstood. Now, in relating this story, I am in no way comparing myself to Milarepa, and certainly I am not comparing the scolding that I received to the actions of Marpa, but as I struggled to find myself in the midst of this scold-

Scoldings

ing-experience, I remembered Milarepa and his quest for the Truth. And in the end, in my case, the entire experience brought me much closer to Guru—much, much closer. And because of that, I can declare that it was a great blessing, a great blessing indeed.

The scolding took place during a Christmas trip that took us to China for three months. We were about three weeks into the trip, visiting our second Chinese city, Xiamen (pronounce Shah-men). Guru had just offered a Peace Concert in the beautiful Botanical Gardens of Xiamen. This event, as it turned out, was the highlight of our Chinese experience.

Without getting too much into the details, I found myself at the end of the concert speaking with a young Chinese, late-teen couple who attended. They were really thrilled with the concert and explained to me and my friend that it is customary to say thank you by offering their services. The young boy was a tour guide and kept offering and offering to take us here and there. We replied with many "No thank you's" as we only had a half hour, and it was really unnecessary for them to do so. At their insistence, we finally set off on a photographic tour of the Botanical Gardens. As we toured the gardens, my friend took pictures here and there, while I walked and talked with the couple who were only too happy to practice their English.

I was really inspired by them. It was the first time I had a real conversation with anyone in China. As China was progressing into the 21st century, their talk was filled with hope for their personal future. After the tour, I commented to friends that the tour was the highlight of my Chinese experience to that point.

Later that afternoon, I was called to the function room. I was anticipating massaging Guru, as had become my regular afternoon duty. Instead, I was greeted with something that was much more shocking. Guru had received a letter from someone "concerned" that I was walking around with a girl for a half hour. It was couched totally with an inappropriate romantic air, and to

Scoldings

punctuate it perfectly, not only was I walking around with a girl, I had the audacity to declare this the "highlight of my trip".

Guru read the letter aloud in front of the entire group. When I realized this was a scolding, I tried to do the right thing. I walked up front and center and stood with hands folded. He then went on to scold me about as ruthlessly as one could be scolded. He brought up all my past mistakes, my past scoldings and told me not to come to any function for three days, clarifying that I could meditate in my room.

Now, allow me to pause here to emphasize again that while I felt the letter as read was a misrepresentation of what actually took place, it does not mean that Guru had no right to scold me, or was incorrect in doing so. Guru would not scold me, or anyone for that matter, merely based on a letter, without getting some inner confirmation from his own Inner Pilot.

Knowing this, I could easily "confess" a thousand legitimate reasons for Guru to scold me. Frankly, there was not a single day in my life that I did not give Guru such cause, and in this instance, the letter may have provided the catalyst that Guru needed. Or perhaps I had simply become complacent in my consciousness, and the scolding provided the kind of jolt to move me forward— a jolt which only a scolding could provide. Or, again, the scolding may have served to expose me to the weakness in my inner character, as evidenced in my experience in the months that followed.

But frankly, in the Guru-student relationship, the Guru is under no obligation to justify his actions to the student, nor should the student demand it. Should the Guru offer an explanation, it is only to further the student's illumination on a mental level. But mental illumination is not the ultimate goal. The goal is life-transformation on every level of one's being. In hindsight, the pain I experienced was all there because my ego and all that it stands for is still very nicely intact! Philosophically, I should welcome anything that exposes that for what it is. As I mentioned earlier, the experience of this scolding ultimately brought me much

Scoldings

closer to Guru. I would readily go through it again, because it ultimately served that higher purpose. Now, back to the scolding.

After what seemed to be an eternity, there was an uncomfortable pause. I asked Guru if he was expecting or wanting a reply from me, to which he said, "fine". I began simply by explaining, "First of all, I wasn't alone, I was with Abakash (my dearest friend), and..." Before I said anything more, Guru cut me off saying, "Then I should also scold Abakash. How could he let you do this kind of thing?"

I realized that the thing to do was just to remain silent. Somewhere in the depth of my heart was a message reminding me of the number of times Guru had told me, "I scold you because I love you. Would I bother to scold a dog in the street?" It would have been even better if I could have smiled, but I couldn't. At Guru's request, I left the room, and then the torture began.

I was so hurt and humiliated. I wanted to move to another hotel, so I wouldn't be seen or have to face anyone. My dearest friend Abakash wisely convinced me that this would be completely wrong. It would have been absolutely perfect if I could have received this scolding with joy, but I could not. I was indignant that my version of "the truth" was never aired. I remained in my room that night, hiding. (This thing called "truth" is a relative thing. In my opinion, until we are fully realized, we all live in a world of relative falsehood.)

The next morning, I made my way to a local café to sit alone. Two disciples came in, Projjwal and his daughter Aruna, both of whom are very, very dear to me. They came and sat with me for a moment.

"Are you okay?"

I nodded.

Projjwal added, "I have to tell you, I needed that scolding. We all felt it. And you can tell everyone was changed after it. But I tell you, I couldn't have taken it had Guru scolded me like that. But that scolding was for all of us."

Scoldings

At that moment, I appreciated the consoling words more than you can imagine, but still found myself wondering that if it was meant for everyone, couldn't Guru have chosen some other instrument?!!

That afternoon brought the next challenge. I went to the dining area where we all ate lunch. The person who wrote the letter approached me. "Pradhan, I wrote the letter." Somehow, I had already known that. "I was only expressing my concern. I had no idea Guru would scold you like that." I smiled, acknowledged her with an "I know," while inwardly I was seething. I roamed through the dining area and was greeted with regular and sympathetic "Heys," "How ya doing's?" accompanied with an uncomfortable timid silence.

A few days later, I received a message from Guru that I could return to the function room, but I could participate in nothing else—no singing, no plays, no races. At first, I found myself attending all the functions, but my inner anger slowly ate away at my enthusiasm for it all. Eventually, the morning meditations were all that I participated in, with an occasional token appearance at the evening functions. Instead of having the best seat in the house at Guru's feet, I sat in the back trying to be as invisible as possible.

On the Christmas trip, every two weeks or so, a large group of people exit the trip and an equal-sized group joins. I was chagrined to learn that my scolding was heard "around the world". With each new group of arrivals, friends would approach me inquiring as to what happened, and offered their own iteration of what they had heard. Like the children's game of 'telephone', apparently with each telling of the scolding, the version got worse and worse. Instead of the inner agony ebbing, it simply intensified with each passing day. I could not wait to get home. There were still weeks left to the trip, and as each day passed, the days became longer and longer. I actually created a little computer program which would flash how many days were left

Scoldings

on the trip whenever I turned my computer on. I couldn't wait for the trip to end.

Finally, the day of departure arrived. Our trip took us from China to Los Angeles. I would normally travel on to New York, but when we arrived in LA, I left the trip and spent a few days with my younger brother. Finally, I made my way home to Chicago.

When I returned home, I felt freer to begin the process of healing than I did while on the trip but, to be frank, I didn't really know if I wanted to. Because my ban on participating in activities had not been officially lifted by Guru, I operated under the same premises when I arrived home. I attended Centre meetings, worked at my restaurant, Victory's Banner, but did nothing else. I felt distance and estrangement from Guru, which was terribly uncomfortable. Before this, in my mind and heart, I would always be thinking and feeling about Guru's needs, but now I wouldn't or couldn't feel the same way, and this caused a crushing pain in my heart.

I remember one incident regarding this. Guru was dear friends with the immortal sitarist Ravi Shankar, and the opportunity came to attend one of his concerts in Philadelphia. Because this was a public event, I felt I could go with the other disciples who attended the concert. After the concert, Guru was standing outside the stage door waiting to meet with Raviji. I saw that he needed a chair and normally would retrieve one and bring it to Guru, but I was so reluctant to do so. This sense of inner intimacy I had now lost, and it pained me deeply.

April Celebrations were approaching. My dearest friend Meghabhuti, (to whom you've already been introduced) came down with a rare auto-immune illness called Guillain-Barre Syndrome. Tragically, this illness causes a temporary paralysis as the auto-immune system attacks the nerves. Fortunately the disease is treatable and recovery is usually 100 percent. At the time, Meghabhuti was paralyzed from the waist down, with additional significant loss of his right arm and facial muscles.

Scoldings

I wanted to visit Meghabhuti before going to New York, but felt I needed special permission to do so, since I was operating under the scolding "you are not to do anything" rule. I called Ashrita who promptly asked Guru. Guru's response was "Why is he asking this? Of course he can go." Ashrita explained that I was still operating under the rules of my scolding. Guru said, "Tell Pradhan I expect only the divine life from him. I expect perfect Perfection and nothing else."

I spent two days in Minneapolis and then made my way to New York for the April Celebrations which were already underway. Guru has a favorite saying, "The past is dust," and so it seemed for Guru as far as I was concerned. I assumed my usual role of massaging Guru and regular evening visits to his home. But the past was not dust for me. I still felt wounded from the scolding and would not allow myself to let go of the experience. Despite the fact that I found myself at my favorite seat, I imposed an inner distance between myself and Guru.

Guru had often publicly declared that I received more brutal scoldings than any other disciple. It is a badge of honor. My friend Sanatan once offered an interesting take on this honor. He consoled me, saying that Guru would love to be able to scold so many disciples, but he can't, either because of his own compassion, or because they wouldn't be able to endure the scolding. He suggested that I was a "vent" for Guru and it was such a valuable service!

Ultimately, many good things evolved from this experience, and one of those things had already begun to show its face. There is one other boy who could compete with me for this honor of "most scolded". His name is Pulak. Both he and I became students in 1971 and lived together at Sarama's house. We were always friends, but as a result of this scolding, we grew much closer. He would speak to me and call me regularly to commiserate. We used to joke that we should write a book called "Letters from the Doghouse," because that is where we would often find ourselves—in Guru's doghouse!

Scoldings

I shared with Pulak an experience which made me smile. Guru had been currently immersed in writing a series of poems called *Seventy-Seven Thousand Service Trees.* They are printed in books of a thousand each, and every time a new book is released (books are still being published after Guru's passing!), as part of our meditation in Chicago, we pass the book around so that each person can spontaneously open to a page and read an aphorism. It's sort of like tossing the coins for the I-Ching. Well, when I opened the book and read my poem, I had to smile…

> "My Lord,
> If You really love me,
> Then You will scold me most ruthlessly
> If I do even the most insignificant thing wrong."

I remembered giggling aloud as I read this.

Guru always referred to Pulak as "my best student," and indeed he was and remanins an ever-present servant. One of his jobs was to drive Guru around for an afternoon meditation drive. I had told Pulak about my aphorism, and for whatever reason, he took the liberty to share this with Guru, as he was driving Guru the next day.

Guru told Pulak to call me immediately with this message. "Tell Pradhan that in my own life, only my own Mother and Aunt could scold me ruthlessly, and I can only scold members of my own family this way. I scold him like this because he is that close to me." I knew Guru saw how wounded I was. He was now performing his healing magic.

When I next came to New York, I requested an interview to clear everything, which Guru granted. One evening at Guru's house, after everyone had left, Guru told me to stay so that we could speak. Guru immediately spoke to me of his expectation of me and that spiritual perfection meant just that. It was all love and all affection. When the moment came, I said to Guru, "But Guru, I miss intimacy."

Scoldings

With this, Guru laughed, and since I was within reach of Guru's foot, he gave me a nice tap with his left foot. "What...intimacy?! How much closer can you be?! Enough now. Now go, all my love, infinite love, infinite love." And with that I smiled and all was well, but the final chapter had not been written on this event.

Perhaps a year later, I was invited to Guru's house one afternoon to massage his legs. Whenever I arrived at Guru's house, I would always first go to the basement to wash my face and hands and then meditate, waiting for Guru's, "Tell him to come and bring the table." When I went downstairs, my spiritual sister Nishtha was there. "Oh Pradhan, Guru was just saying how much he loved you!"

Surprised and delighted, I asked how it was that the subject should have turned to me. Nishtha explained, "I was giving Guru a video tape, and he inquired what it was. I told him it was a video of the Xiamen Peace Concert from China. He said, 'Oh that...that is where that thing happened with Pradhan. And then I ruined his entire vacation. I tell you, how much I love that boy.'"

I couldn't believe my ears. As I mentioned earlier, that particular event, the Peace Concert in Xiamen, was the highlight of Guru's visit to China. This is what I would have expected Guru to remember. But no! Of all the things to remember, Guru remembered my scolding.

On October 11, 2007, my Guru, my Beloved Guru, left this world, or as he would say, he "passed behind the curtain of Eternity". No more scoldings. How I wish he were here, so that I could receive them once again.

10

The Final Chapter

Of all the moments I have had with Guru, this one strikes me as one of the most precious, and in my own life I return to it over and over again. Frankly, I feel it belongs to everyone.

❖ **"You belong to me"**
On the last day of a visit to New York, I was at Guru's home, and I asked Guru if I might be able to speak to him privately for just a few minutes. Guru kindly accommodated my request; so later that afternoon, Guru cleared the immediate area and said, "Now, tell me what, good boy?"

"Guru," I said, " I am surrounded by the darkness of failure. Everything you have asked me to do, I have failed at. The Centre hasn't met your expectations, I had to close the restaurant (the first Victory's Banner) and no concert has succeeded the way you wanted it to. I don't know...I'm just depressed. Failure is the only thing I see in my life."

The Final Chapter

"No, no, it is not like that," Guru replied sweetly. "Think of the farmer. He takes the garden...the soil can be very dry. And what does he do? He fertilizes the soil. Now, you cannot say that the fertilizer is very beautiful. All the time he works the soil and fertilizes the soil. Only then does it develop into a most beautiful garden.

"Or, think of the potter molding a lump of clay. He takes the clay and shapes it into something beautiful. But all the time while he is molding the clay, it is not very beautiful."

Guru went on, explaining most patiently.

"Right now, the Supreme is molding you into something beautiful. These things that you see as failures are only stepping stones to something more beautiful."

Then, with utmost sweetness and affection, Guru added, "Finally, if all these things should fail you, just remember this. You belong to me...you belong to me."

About the Author

Pradhan Balter is a chiropractor, a computer consultant, and owns a vegetarian restaurant and flower store in Chicago. Perhaps more relevant to this book, he has studied meditation for some 40 years with Indian spiritual Teacher Sri Chinmoy. Pradhan serves as director of the Chicago Sri Chinmoy Centre, and has lectured across the United States and in some 40 countries abroad.

In his role as chiropractor, he would regularly sit with his spiritual Teacher working on the Master's ever-present knee and leg pain, and much of the stories and experiences contained within this book are drawn from this special relationship.

Pradhan is available to speak to groups of any size about meditation. His down-to-earth style and light-hearted approach makes meditation both accessible and inspiring. There is never a charge nor are donations ever accepted for such events.

Contact Pradhan

e-mail: pradhan@atthefeetofmymaster.com
address: Pradhan Balter
c/o Victory's Banner
2100 W. Roscoe St.
Chicago, IL 60618
web: http://atthefeetofmymaster.com

Other books by Pradhan

If you are interested in meditation, or trying to live a more spiritual life in today's fast-paced world, you'll enjoy

A 21st-Century Seeker

A 21st-Century Seeker can serve as an inspiring self-help book for anyone who wants to learn meditation, or it can work as a teaching guide for a class or group. For more information, visit www.atthefeetofmymaster.com/21st_century.

www.ingramcontent.com/pod-product-compliance
Lightning Source LLC
Chambersburg PA
CBHW071706040426
42446CB00011B/1933